Presidents, Secretaries of State, and Crises in U.S. Foreign Relations

Other Titles in This Series

Westview Special Studies in International Relations and U.S. Foreign Policy

Presidents, Secretaries of State, and
Crises in U.S. Foreign Relations:
A Model and Predictive Analysis
Lawrence S. Falkowski

This book presents a new approach to analyzing the impact of individuals on U.S. foreign policy, and reports the results of this analysis for all post-World War II presidents and secretaries of state, including President Carter and Secretary of State Vance. Its compelling but fundamentally simple theme suggests that it may be unnecessary to adopt traditional models of psychology in order to predict the behavior of foreign-policy decision makers. Earlier studies based on these models are either too judgmental to be predictively useful or too abstract to be relevant to the policy process itself. In contrast, the underlying assumption here is that the information necessary to make accurate predictions is more easily obtainable and understandable than once thought.

The methods employed to test Dr. Falkowski's predictive model are easy to understand and to replicate. The results indicate a strong relationship between variations in the memories of leaders and their abilities to adopt flexible courses of action when faced with crisis situations. This relationship exists for all presidents and secretaries of state studied, suggesting that it is possible to predict the behavior of new or potential leaders before they are faced with crisis decisions. The implications of these results are far-reaching and might be directly applicable to the selection of new leaders.

Lawrence S. Falkowski is assistant professor of political science at Louisiana State University, where he specializes in the fields of international politics and foreign policy. Dr. Falkowski is author of a major foreign policy text, *Beyond the National Interest: Toward a New Understanding of Foreign Policy.*

Presidents, Secretaries of State, and Crises in U.S. Foreign Relations: A Model and Predictive Analysis

Lawrence S. Falkowski

Westview Press/Boulder, Colorado

Westview Special Studies in
International Relations and U.S. Foreign Policy

CI   JUL. 1 0 1979

Copyright © 1978 by Westview Press, Inc.

Published in 1978 in the United States of America by
   Westview Press, Inc.
   5500 Central Avenue
   Boulder, Colorado 80301
   Frederick A. Praeger, Publisher

Library of Congress Cataloging in Publication Data
Falkowski, Lawrence S.
   Presidents, secretaries of state, and crises in U.S. foreign relations.
   (Westview special studies in international relations and foreign policy)
   Based on the author's thesis.
   1. United States—Foreign relations—1945—Research. 2. International relations—Research. 3. United States—Foreign relations administration.
   I. Title.
JX1417.F34   327.73   77-27049
ISBN 0-89158-072-7
ISBN 0-89158-073-5 pbk.

Printed and bound in the United States of America

To my wife Carol

Feelings dwell in man;
but man dwells in his love.
—Martin Buber

Contents

Tables

Acknowledgments

A book is never the product of individual effort. In its final form, it represents a unique combination of insights drawn from many people and many events. I would like, therefore, to thank those who helped this book grow to maturity. Several scholars aided this work, and they deserve special thanks: Professors Charles Jacob, Yale Ferguson, and Warren Sussman. The book began as a dissertation, and mention should be made of Richard Mansbach, the supervisor of that early process. Professor Donald E. Lampert must be singled out not only for his scholarly support, suggestions, and insights, but also for his ability to ask life's hard questions with compassion and humor. The final version of the manuscript was prepared at Louisiana State University, and appreciation and thanks are due to the members of the political science department, the graduate school, and my research assistants Paul Lambert and Clara Garza Leach.

I also wish to thank Lynne Rienner and Frederick Praeger, without whose confidence and support this work would not have been printed. Last and most important, Carol Falkowski deserves special thanks and praise for her ability to tolerate all the trials and tribulations connected with this project.

1
Introduction

In 1803 Thomas Jefferson urged the immediate ratification of a treaty usually referred to as the "Louisiana Purchase."[1] He had earlier contended that the central government should do as little as possible and that when it did act, it should do so only within the strictest construction of the constitution. Jefferson had claimed to be a supporter of passive government. "I am not," he said, "a friend of very energetic government."[2] Jefferson's first inaugural address, delivered only two years before the Louisiana Purchase, had a similar message: "Still one thing more, fellow-citizens—a wise and frugal Government shall restrain man from injuring one another, shall leave them otherwise free to regulate their own pursuits."[3]

If this is indicative of Jefferson's attitude toward central government, how could such a great change occur in so short a time? How could a supporter of "frugal" government urge—only two years later—the spending of twelve million dollars to purchase land that extended from the Mississippi River to the Rocky Mountains? How could a man who believed in a strict construction of the constitution now be willing to spend money for the annexation of land when the Constitution did not provide for annexation?

Perhaps Jefferson saw France's closing of the Mississippi as so great a threat that he had no choice but to pursue a novel policy. Perhaps, if he were to be consistent to his beliefs, he had to protect the yeoman farmer—whom he believed to be the foundation of the republic; perhaps, in order to protect them, he had to protect the shipping lanes in the Mississippi. Perhaps, in order to protect the Mississippi, he had to change his policy from little international activity to major negotiations. All this is sheer speculation, but some support for such reasoning may be found in Jefferson's own statements. On September 20, 1810, he wrote, "To lose our country by a scrupulous adherence to the written law, would be to lose the law itself, with life, liberty and property and all those who are enjoying them with us; thus absurdly sacrificing the ends to the means."[4]

It may seem rather odd for Jefferson, who feared the Federalists as monarchists in disguise, to take for himself a privilege that could be considered tyrannical at best. One of the major values in his philosophy was respect for the written law, but the statement cited above seems to contradict that. Jefferson's approach to the Louisiana Purchase was something between demagoguery and true statesmanship. Whatever his motives may have been, it would be fair to conclude that faced with a precarious and extremely novel situation, Jefferson changed his foreign policy.

This characterization of Jefferson's behavior—it is, of course, a superficial characterization—nevertheless shows what is needed for a proper investigation of his foreign policy: a research design that includes elements of political science, sociology, psychology, and history. If Jefferson were the only type of person who held high office in the United States, then our task might be somewhat easier, for we could look at elements common to all leaders and hypothesize that some common factor in their backgrounds was responsible for their changing policies. Clearly, though, not all leaders display the same qualities as Jefferson.

John Foster Dulles, who served as secretary of state (a post that Jefferson also held) in the 1950s, is usually viewed as extremely inflexible in his attitudes and behavior toward the Soviet Union.[5] It is claimed, in fact, that Dulles was so set against the Soviets that no amount of contradictory information could change his outlook or his behavior. When the Soviet Union planned to reduce its armed forces by 1,200,000 men, Dulles refused to concede that the reduction might reduce tensions. He was asked, "Isn't it a fair conclusion from what you [Dulles] have said this morning that you would prefer to have the Soviet Union keep these men in their armed forces?" Dulles replied, "Well it's a fair conclusion that I would rather have them standing around doing guard duty than making atomic bombs."[6] In addition, Ole Holsti suggests, Dulles changed his behavior little if at all during his tenure as secretary of state. He exhibited this inflexibility in both crisis and non-crisis situations.

These striking illustrations suggest certain differences among those who have played leadership roles in the United States government and the great differences in the responses that they have made. If leaders do exhibit behavior that differs in the direction and intensity of change, how can we measure the direction and intensity of this type of behavior?

This book addresses the problem of a leader's ability to change directions in foreign policy situations, that is, both to change the policies themselves and the objectives sought. Some people have called this type of behavior *learning, adaptation,* or *flexibility.* Regardless of the term used, the concept is central to any analysis of foreign policy. Just as it is important in business to know whether a given client is a tough or easy bargainer, the student of U.S. foreign policy should have some idea of the tendency of a president or secretary of state to change direction if the situation warrants it. Flexibility is of course a basic element in anyone's personality. The problem is, however, that scholars differ in their approach to this kind of directional change. If the term *learn* is used, it usually means that a person has changed from a less to a more desirable behavior. If the term *adaptiveness* or *adaptation* is employed, the same normative implication can be drawn. Yet the concept of change alone does not convey the type of behavior difference that seems important in the study of foreign policy. *Change* may be viewed as any behavior that is not completely congruent with previous behavior. In order to use terminology that will convey the notion of change, without major value implications, I have adopted the term *flexibility*. In this context, *flexibility* is defined as a change in observed behavior from a previous pattern of behavior; it is quite similar to *adaptiveness* but does not have the normative implications of that term.

The degree and direction of change or flexibility are very important. If a leader intensifies a certain action, it may be considered a change, yet it indicates a rather low degree of flexibility. For example, consider a leader who decides to step up bombing activities against the enemy. The increase in bombs dropped and missions flown indicates *some* type of change, but in the absence of additional information, it tells us little about flexibility. If, however, the same leader completely changes his tactics—for example, by stopping the bombing runs and beginning peace talks—we may be able to view that as indicative of flexible behavior.

The concept of flexibility is a rather important variable in terms of foreign policy, since we know that in certain situations leaders may have an extremely important role in determining the direction of that policy.[7] Namely, these situations are when the stakes of the game are extremely high—that is, they are crises. In normal times (non-crisis), to be sure, other variables may be more important in explaining policy formulation and execution. But in a crisis, the possibility of a situation's returning to normal is limited unless the crisis is successfully dealt with.

One task of this study will be to develop a scale that can differentiate among various degrees of flexibility. If we are successful in defining and operationalizing flexibility, then we may be able to answer the question: are some leaders more flexible than others? Another significant question is: what variables are related to the degree of flexibility of leaders' behavior?

The questions will be examined in the following manner. First, the problem will be discussed in the context of foreign policy research and theory. Second, a framework for analysis will be constructed, one that is based on the insights obtained from the examination of these materials; from this framework, we will derive certain hypotheses. Third, I will offer a research design to operationalize the concepts contained within the framework and to test the hypotheses that have been generated.

The Utility of Perceptions, Memory, and Motivation in Foreign Policy

The central question in this study is the flexibility of U.S. foreign policymakers. Do U.S. leaders exhibit flexibility in foreign policy situations? Second, do different leaders exhibit different degrees of flexibility? Third, what factors are related to a leader's flexibility or inflexibility?

In order to examine these questions, a research design will be presented that tests the degree of flexibility in a situation where the probability of flexible response is at its highest. In order to examine any of the questions listed, we first must have some idea of what flexibility is. For purposes of this research, I will consider flexibility in terms of foreign policy goals and objectives. To examine goals and objectives, I have constructed a framework that suggests how goals and objectives are linked to situations and motivations.

Motivation, Perception, and Goals

A fundamental question in the examination of flexibility is motivation. Although we are not attempting to create a causal model of flexibility, we must be aware of theories of motivation that link stimulus and response in ways that might be useful. Thus, the first question becomes, why do men act, or what motivates certain types of action? According to C. N. Cofer and M. H. Appley, motivation is composed of three basic elements:

8   *Perceptions, Memory, and Motivation*

(1) an environmental determinant which precipitate[s] the behavior in question—the application of some irresistible force
which of necessity . . . [led] to this action; (2) the internal
urge, wish, feeling, emotion, drive, instinct, want, desire,
demand, purpose, interest, aspiration, plan, need or motive
which [gives] rise to the action; or (3) the incentive, goal, or
object value which attract[s] or repel[s] the organism.[1]

With this description in mind, it is relatively easy to see
the part that goals and objectives can play. A *goal* is a desired
future situation, and a *policy* is a concrete action taken to
achieve the goal. Elements two and three of the description
seem to fit nicely into this framework. The problem occurs
with the first factor. By the use of the term *environmental
determinant,* one might assume that the "real" environment
is being referred to. But Cofer and Appley here appear to be
saying that some inexorable force leads to an action.

Several other authors also suggest that it is not objective
reality, but rather the perception of that reality, that is crucial for individual motivations. Harold and Margaret Sprout
describe the role of perception as follows:

what matters in shaping human attitudes and decisions [and in
explaining these] is not how the real world actually is, but
rather how it is perceived or imagined to be by the individuals
under consideration . . . what is perceived is interpreted in the
light of past experiences, individuals with different backgrounds may interpret quite differently the same perceived
objects or events.[2]

John P. Lovell makes a similar point. He, however, having
taken the Sprouts' insights, argues that an individual's belief
system will cause him to filter out certain information that
does not support his belief or ideas.

It is not only the laymen whose vision is limited and who per-
ceive and interpret phenomena selectively on the basis of their

values and beliefs. Policy makers, too, are susceptible to intellectual blindness and to distortions of view; historical and contemporary examples of the judgements of policy makers being distorted through the interplay of their values and beliefs are abundant.[3]

This subject of perception is also emphasized by Karl W. Deutsch in his use of selections and abstractions as a means by which the individual is able to handle incoming information.[4] But perhaps the best description of the role of perception as related to foreign policy is given by Holsti, North, and Brody:

> The key concept . . . is the *perception,* the process by which decision-makers detect and assign meaning to inputs from their environment and formulate their own purposes and intents. For an individual to respond to a person, object, or event, there must first be the *detection* of signals, which is a function of our senses. In addition, however, we must have some code— a set of concepts of images—which permit us to interpret the meaning of the stimulus.[5]

Thus the "environmental determinant" can be viewed in terms of a given organism's perception of that determinant. This study assumes that perception, values, objectives, and policies are interrelated. Since perception is crucial to the entire decision-making process, it therefore becomes crucial to this study, precisely because a stimulus that is not perceived cannot set in motion the other elements mentioned above and therefore cannot lead to observable behavior. Thus, to the degree that individuals' perceptions differ, I hypothesize that their behavior will also differ, and perception becomes an important variable in the discussion of flexibility. For if an organism perceives an event as beneficial, it will probably behave in a very different manner than if it perceives the event as threatening.

Two major tasks, therefore, are to create a model of

flexible foreign policy behavior and to examine how flexibility is related to different foreign policy statements and behavior. Once a theoretical link among perception, goals, and objectives is established, a research design can be created that enables us to test various hypotheses derived from that model.

Decision Making and Foreign Policy Analysis

At first glance, the decision-making approach to the study of international politics and foreign policy seems to offer a valuable source of information and insight into the role that a flexible leader might play in foreign policy. The assumptions of decision-making analysis are similar to our later assumptions. For example, decision-making analysis assumes that the decision-maker is important and that decisions are part of a process based to some degree on information flows.

Since decision making is involved in information processes, many authors tend to link aspects of communications theory with the decision-making process. Hopkins and Mansbach view decision making in the following manner: "Past experience shapes an individual's or an organization's image of the environment and influences responses to current information. Memory not only fills in missing pieces of information as it organizes perceptions but also facilitates interpretation of those perceptions. Memory affects current decisions in the form of feedback inputs."[6] These same authors view foreign policy as "the product of decisions by relevant individuals in a complex organizational setting."[7] Patrick Morgan, taking a systems analysis view of the foreign policy process, nevertheless still views the decision-making process and the decision-maker as central to foreign policy. He states, "for purposes of research the nation is at any given time its decision-makers."[8] Since he also uses elements of communication theory in his discussion of decision making, he makes memory, information flows, and feedback important to a decision-making structure.[9] Harold and Margaret Sprout agree with Morgan's position that decision making is important to foreign policy and to what they call "international actions." They claim that the "essence of undertakings is decision-making."[10] (If the Sprouts are correct, we can then understand foreign behavior by closely examining how a given actor makes decisions.)

The Sprouts' statement is given further support by Charles F. Hermann and Roger Hilsman. Hermann states, "Foreign Policy results from the decision-makers' perceptions of present or expected problems in the relationships between a nation and its international environment [both human and nonhuman]."[11] Hilsman makes the same point speaking in an American context: "The business of Washington is making decisions that move a nation, decisions about the direction American society should take and decisions about how and where and for what purpose the awesome power—economic, political, and military—of this nation shall be used."[12]

Thus, in spite of specific differences, all these authors believe that decision making is, in general, important and vital to the understanding of foreign policy in particular. If this approach is useful (and it does seem to contain some interesting insights), then it might be useful to determine how widespread it is in the study of foreign policy. Yet even when we expand the definition to include elements of communications theory (for example, memory, feedback, perception), we still find that little has been published on these topics.[13]

The unit of analysis in the decision-making approach is the individual decision. Scholars who use this approach tend to concentrate upon variables such as the structure of a decision-making apparatus or the group loyalties of the individual decision-maker. By examining these, they hope to explain and predict decisions (outputs) by a careful analysis of the nature and content of inputs. The problem inherent in the decision-making literature, however, is that it usually assumes that a decision-maker will act rationally, that is, that he or she will choose the best of all possible alternatives. This assumption cannot be fully supported, since decision-makers usually have only limited information.[14] Another problem with decision-making analysis is that it tends to ignore the fact that even given the same information, decision-makers may act in very different ways regardless of role. This may be attributable to different perceptions or a different set of priorities or values. Thus objective rationality cannot be used as a device for understanding how a decision-maker is likely to act.

Several authors have dealt with this problem of the rationality of a leader's action. Some examine the problem by testing the effect of certain psychological variables upon individuals or governments or both. Using content analysis, for example, North and Choucri,[15] Holsti,[16] Holsti, North, and Brody,[17] M. D. Wallace,[18] and Maurice A. East[19] have examined the relationship between status, status discrepancies, and other psychological variables, on one hand, and the international behavior of actors on the other. Other authors have borrowed very heavily from psychology. De Rivera[20] and Janis[21] both use psychological metaphors and insights to explain how decisions are reached. Janis develops his theory of "groupthink" and then uses decisions reached in historic crises to illustrate his theory. De Rivera assumes that there is a psychological dimension to foreign policy and then uses historical examples to support his assumption.

All these approaches, however, lack clarity and focus, both in terms of perception and behavior. Even though many authors believe that both the perceptions and the decision-making process are important to a full understanding of foreign policy formation, little work has been done on linking these two variables. Rather, many authors (Graham Allison is a prime example)[22] try to create decision-making models. Still others attempt intensive case studies of one or two situations in order to discover what has "really" happened so that they can make generalizations.[23] Such efforts to understand foreign policy have on balance yielded rather disappointing results. Even though each case study may be excellent in itself, the various studies, owing in large measure to the lack of a single organizing theory, have not led to a cumulative and coherent body of knowledge.

In addition to the lack of cumulative knowledge, a second, and perhaps more interesting, problem has also been overlooked. The assumption of rationality in decision making must be questioned in light of the research done on perception. If rationality means to choose the best of all possible alternatives, then we must know what is "best" in order to determine whether the decision was rational. But the best alternative is a subjective judgment. Depending upon the perceptions of a given decision-maker, the best decision may be one that protects his career or his agency or his government. Unless it can be determined which of several motives are most salient to the decision-maker, it becomes exceedingly difficult to speak in objective terms of the most "rational" decision.

Models of Decision Making

Most research on decision making begins with a theoretical framework that tries to relate the variables considered important in decision making. One of the earliest models of decision making was that of Richard C. Snyder, H. W. Bruck, and Burton Sapin.[24] They identified five clusters factors considered to be important: (1) internal setting of decision making, (2) social structure and behavior, (3) decision-making process—decision-makers, (4) action, (5) external setting of decision making. In addition to these factors, Snyder et al. contend that the definition of a situation is important to the entire decision-making process: "The key to the explanation of why the state behaves the way it does lies in the way its decision-makers as actors define their situation."[25] Decision-makers are oriented to these definitions by

the interplay of three elements: "perception, choice, and expectation."[26] What this formulation proposes is a mediated
response model but without operational definitions of several
of their factors.[27] According to James N. Rosenau, however,
decision-making analysis in general has not been investigated
because Snyder's original formulation and later suggestions
for research lack "if-then" hypotheses.[28] (There are several
reasons for this, not the least of which is that decision making may be too broad to be examined as a whole and second
that the adoption of elements of psychological socialization
research requires that the political scientist become a compe-
tent psychologist.)[29]

Whatever the shortcomings of the Snyder model, it did
lead to further research on decision making. Many authors
focused on one or another element of the model, and others
concentrated on different types of situations. Still others
created competing decision-making models and tested them
in specific situations. A summary of these various approaches
should indicate the diversity of opinion and eclecticism that
has developed in the field.

Patrick M. Morgan claims that most decision-makers rely
on introspection to make decisions.[30] Others who view perception as key to the process include Ernest May,[31] Harold
and Margaret Sprout,[32] John Lovell,[33] and Ole Holsti et al.[34]
Charles Hermann and those who do crisis research are involved in Snyder's model—by implication at least—in claiming
that the situation is an important explanatory variable in
decision making. The work of Hermann,[35] Paige,[36] Robinson
and Snyder,[37] and Alexander George[38] can be viewed in this
manner. Perhaps the most outstanding example of competing
models has been offered by Graham Allison, whose three
models were applied to the Cuban missile crisis.[39] James
McCormick's later tests of models of crisis behavior can be
viewed in terms of both competing models of decision
making and situational variables that may affect the way in
which decisions are made.[40]

In short, a review of the analysis that has been done on "decision making" has left many important questions unanswered. The first is the role of the individual in the decision-making process. Are individuals important at all, and, if so, how do they affect foreign policy decisions and behavior? How are perceptions, situations, and motivations linked? In addition we must investigate the question of change and how change occurs without defining each decision as a completely new situation.

In order to address these problems, it is first necessary to determine when and under what conditions individuals are likely to be important in the formation of foreign policy. This step is crucial, because no matter how well constructed a model of motivation and perception of individuals may be, if individuals have no impact on the foreign policy process, we have not added any explanatory power to our analysis of foreign policy.

The Role of the Individual in Foreign Policy

The literature on decision making suggests that individuals ultimately make the decisions. This does not mean, however, that the study of individuals is the best way to understand how foreign policy is made. If individuals are constrained by various factors, then the study of those factors becomes the most important, and the individuals become rather irrelevant, since any individual in that position would perform in the same fashion. The factors that may be important in determining an individual's behavior must be examined in terms of the factors themselves and the situations in which decisions are reached.

What, then, are the factors that may be important in an analysis of foreign policy? James N. Rosenau suggests that five variable clusters are likely to be important in foreign policy: role, societal, governmental, systemic, and individual.[41] In different types of countries, he maintains, different variable clusters are likely to be more or less potent.[42] In

larger underdeveloped countries, for example, whether they
are open or closed societies, individual variables are likely to
be most important; in small underdeveloped countries, individual variables will also be most important.[43]

If Rosenau's "pre-theory" is accurate, then many Third
World countries will exhibit foreign policies that can be explained best by examining the individual. The logic used to
support this formulation need not concern us at this point.
What is important is the definition of the individual variable
cluster.

> The first set [variable cluster] encompasses the characteristics
> unique to the decision-makers who determine and implement
> the foreign policies of a nation. Individual variables include all
> those aspects of a decision-maker—his values, talents, and prior
> experiences—that distinguish his foreign policy choices or be-
> havior from those of every other decision-maker. John Foster
> Dulles' religious values, de Gaulle's vision of a glorious France,
> and Khrushchev's political skills are frequently mentioned
> examples of individual variables.[44]

In Rosenau's view, therefore, the individual may have an
impact on foreign policy, especially in "underdeveloped"
countries. Although few hard data support this claim, it
seems intuitively obvious in light of the foreign policy of
countries such as Uganda. However, as noted, our focus is on
decision-makers in the United States, which is not underdeveloped. Therefore, we cannot assume that the individual
variable cluster will be the most important.

The next question is whether individual variables in large,
developed open societies have an impact on foreign policy.
Although Rosenau would claim that the role variable cluster
has the most explanatory power in these countries and that
the individual cluster is the least important,[45] he does state
that all the variable clusters are important for the formulation of foreign policy. On the other hand, researchers who
adopt the operational code approach to explain individual

and group behavior assume that individual variables are important to policy formulation regardless of the nature of the government involved.[46] They contend that the attitudes and perceptions of certain leaders can be translated into foreign policies of the countries they represent. If a leader is in a position of authority in which the role constraints are not great and in which pressure from society is modified, then his individual personality is likely to have an impact on the foreign policy decision. This contention seems logical enough, but Rosenau's caveat would be that such circumstances are unlikely to arise in a large developed open society such as the United States. We must thus determine if there is any situation in which individual variables are likely to be important.

Individual Variables in Crisis Situations

In a crisis, the stakes are high and the time in which decisions are made is short. But a more precise definition of crisis is needed in a discussion of the importance of individual variables. Although there is some controversy about the definition of crisis,[47] the definition used by Hermann is accepted by many scholars and will be adopted here:

> a crisis is a situation that (1) threatens high-priority goals of a decision-making unit, (2) restricts the amount of time available for response before the decision is transformed, and (3) surprises the members of the decision-making unit by its occurrence. Threat, time, and surprise all have been cited as traits of crisis. . . . Underlying the proposed definition is the hypothesis that if all three traits are present then the decision process will be substantially different than if only one or two of the characteristics appear.[48]

In slightly different form, this definition has been employed by many researchers. According to Robinson and Snyder, crisis and crisis decisions have the following attributes: crisis decisions "arise without prior planning, allow short time for response, and have high value consequences."[49] Glenn D.

Paige also adopts the Hermann definition in his research on the Korean decision[50] (in a later article, he uses a similar method of crisis definition by examining time, threat, and surprise as independent variables[51]), and Thomas Brewer has operationalized Hermann's definition.[52] Once we accept the elements of the definition of crisis, we can then examine whether a crisis is a situation in which individual variables are likely to be important. In the last sentence of his definition, Hermann suggests that the decision process may be substantially changed in crisis situations. This contention is given some support by the work of Ernest May.[53] May discusses the apparent paradox in the United States' actions and attitudes toward Korea in 1950, which he explains in terms of two policies for Korea. One was arrived at by reflection, contemplation, and calculation, and the other (which took hold during the crisis) was based on an historical axiom or analogy. As May puts it:

> In June, when the North Koreans launched their attack, the President and his advisers did not judge the event in terms of this [the calculated] policy. Instead, their minds flew to an axiom—that any armed aggression anywhere constituted a threat to all nations everywhere. President Truman writes that while on the plane his mind dwelt on other occasions "when the strong had attacked the weak."[54]

The crucial factor for May is that this axiom is of individual or group invention and tends to be used in crises. May's work suggests the importance of the individual in crises. It is the individual who employs the axiom—whether the axiom itself is of his own invention or is generally accepted by some group. As long as the individual has the choice of axiom and as long as the axiom is used to define the current situation and influence or control his decision, the axiom is inherently dangerous. As May remarks:

> [An axiom's] sources are nearly always historical. Some have
> roots that go very deep. . . . The axiomatic policy that gov-
> erned the Korean decision . . . is derived from the experiences
> of the 1930's. . . . Moreover, while historical experience is the
> substance of an axiom, it is not the molder. People read into
> history more or less what they want to read, and they exercise
> some discretion about the precepts they apply to particular
> cases.[55]

At this point a more detailed discussion of the interplay of
psychology, perception, and crisis components may provide
further insights into the role of individual decision-makers in
crises. We must determine what mechanism is at work during
a crisis and how it affects the decision process. We must also
examine the possibility that in a crisis the individual decision-
maker becomes the most salient explanatory variable in relation to other variable clusters.

The propositions of Fred I. Greenstein are fruitful sources
of comparison with the Hermann definition of crisis, if
we remember that our main interest is in high-level decision-
makers.[56] Since this is the case, we need some idea of what
position a leader has, especially since his position involves
foreign policy decisions in which the stakes may be very high.
Even when there is no crisis, leaders have a high degree of
personal involvement in their positions.[57]

An additional concern in any discussion of leadership is
to what degree the responses of a leader are determined by
role expectation and to what degree they are attributable
to personality factors. In this area there is some disagreement, albeit a qualified disagreement. James N. Rosenau, in
examining decision-making analysis, finds that motives are
important, but that the "in order to" motive seems more important than the "because of" motive.[58] He further states
that in certain situations the "because of" motive may have
an impact on the process itself.[59]

It is curious that Rosenau sees "because of" motives as

those "he [the decision-maker] develops as an individual in a vast array of prior experiences during childhood and adulthood."[60] The curiosity arises in the context of perception. Rosenau seems to be indicating that the "because of" motive is basically idiosyncratic and that the "in order to" motives are basically role-oriented. Yet these distinctions are more artificial than real. One cannot separate the role from the idiosyncratic in terms of perception because what is role today becomes part of memory tomorrow. Rosenau's distinction is not completely applicable here. Since we compare individuals who are in similar roles, the differences in their behavior, therefore, cannot be explained by the fact that they occupy different roles. Merely controlling for role, however, is not the most satisfactory means of supporting an argument that states that individual variables may be important in crisis decision making. Greenstein, for example, suggests that leadership roles allow individual differences to be important.[61] In proposition 11 he states that "personality variations will be more evident to the degree that the individual occupies a position free 'from elaborate expectations of fixed content.' Typically these are leadership positions."[62] This proposition Greenstein supports by citing the work of William Wilcox on the flexibility of military leadership.[63] He adds further support by a discussion of Daniel Levinson's work on roles[64] and concludes that decision-makers toward the top of the decision-making structure have a personal impact on the decisions that are made. Since presidents and secretaries of state are at the top of the decision-making structure, they have very few role constraints and fulfill the requirement of a position "free from elaborate expectations of fixed content."

Hermann states that one of the three elements of crisis is threat. Robinson and Snyder define threat as "high value consequences,"[65] and Greenstein in his proposition 8 states that "The more demanding the political act—the more it is one that calls for an active investment of effort the greater

the likelihood that it will be influenced by personal charac-
teristics of the actor."[66] Both the shortness of time and the
concept of surprise suggest that a great deal of information
must be processed quickly. In his discussion of personality
variables, Greenstein again states:

> Ambiguous situations leave room for personal variability to
> manifest itself . . . three types of ambiguous situations [are]
> (a) the "completely new situation in which there are no famil-
> iar cues" . . . (b) "a complex situation in which there are a
> great number of cues to be taken into account" . . . (c) "a con-
> tradictory situation in which different elements suggest dif-
> ferent structures."[67]

These propositions, which Greenstein supports by reference
to the general psychological literature, are entirely congruent
with the Hermann definition of crisis.[68] Crises are "un-
planned" events during which the need for information increases dramatically. Decision-makers seek information upon
which to make decisions, decisions that must be made within
a limited time or else the situation is likely to change in un-
favorable ways. Assuming that some information is available,
an analogy can help simplify the information and allow conclusions to be drawn quickly. This contention is supported
by Paige, when he states that "crisis tends to be accompanied
by increased search behaviors for new information about the
threatening event and the greater the crisis, the more information about it tends to be elevated to the top of the organizational hierarchy."[69] Paige also suggests that in a crisis, a
propensity to supplement information with past experience
increases as the crisis intensifies.[70]

Thus if we compare Paige's and Greenstein's propositions
and apply both to Hermann's definition of crisis, the following logic suggests itself. In a crisis time is short and an element of surprise is present. In that situation, the decision-
maker will seek as much information as possible and supplement that information with past experience. In effect,

personal experience becomes an inexpensive and available source of information. The assumption is that the information collected will inform the decision-maker as to what historical precedent is available and that the past experience will indicate what incoming information is most relevant and how it should be interpreted. The cues coming in to the decision-makers fit well with Greenstein's concern with ambiguity. Because of surprise, the crisis offers a new situation with no familiar cues; because of the increased demand for information, a great number of cues must be taken into account; finally, the cues may suggest various precedents.

The reason why a decision-maker may seek to supplement current information with historical precedent can be explained in many different ways. One possibility is that in a crisis the decision-maker may be aware of what is taking place but not why it is taking place. What is missing are the motives of another decision-maker. The decision-maker may then attempt to find a historical analogy in which similar events occurred, because he is aware of the motives that were present in a historical situation. The analogy is completed when the decision-maker assumes that the same or similar motives are present in the current situation. This abstract formulation can be illustrated (among other examples) by the example of the Cuban missile crisis. Robert Kennedy and Dean Acheson had access to virtually the same information, and yet the analogies that suggested themselves to them were different.[71] It can be assumed that the chief decision-maker was aware of the different analogies suggested by his subordinates.

Having established the links between psychology and crisis, we see that in a crisis certain individuals are likely to have some impact. It has also been demonstrated that owing to the novelty of the situation, role impact is likely to be relatively minor for leaders. In terms of societal variables and governmental variables, time is so constrained that normal processes of consultation are restricted. Thus, the individual decision-maker is "on his own" without the opportunity to consult with his colleagues in his department or wait for public reaction to the crisis. In short, save for some factual information, the decision-maker and the decision-making group must rely almost completely upon their own resources for analysis, interpretation, and decision in crises.

What I have sought to demonstrate up to this point is that individual variables are likely to be important in crises. I have also indicated some psychological variables that are likely to be important to the individuals involved in a given situation. (This is not to say that in other situations individual variables may not be important.) By implication, then, the questions raised about the flexibility of presidents and secretaries of state take on greater importance in crises. The reaction of Kennedy to the Cuban missile crisis, Truman to Korea, and Eisenhower to the Hungarian uprising illustrate the degree to which the attitudes of these individuals shaped the response of the United States government to these crises.

Central to the question of perception is the information an individual receives. In order for him to respond to a situation, he must be aware that a situation exists. If a decision-maker is not aware of the situation, he cannot respond to it— for him, there is no situation. However, even if a decision-maker is taking in information, his own "perceptual set" may filter out many crucial facts, so that the information he actually receives is very different from the reports that were submitted for his consideration. If this same decision-maker receives only information that reinforces his attitudes and perceptions about other individuals and situations, he will be incapable of flexible behavior. He will be convinced that the situations that are occurring do not require any rethinking on his part.

The ways in which individuals use these filters to sort and process information is central to our problem. These information flows (or "feedback") are adapted from communica-

tions theory. The next task, therefore, is to discuss how the
notion of feedback informs the notion of flexibility.

Communications Theory, Feedback, and Flexibility

The essence of communication is the flow of information. Communications theory is based upon information
flows in and out of an organism. *Feedback,* a particular type
of information flow, can be defined as that flow of information by which the effects of a prior action of the organism
are assessed. Feedback is of two basic types, positive or negative. *Positive,* sometimes called *amplifying* feedback, indicates to the organism that the original action should continue
or be reinforced. *Negative,* or *corrective* feedback, indicates
to the organism that the original action had undesirable
effects and that future action should therefore be altered.

These basic definitions seem to have little relationship to
individual flexibility. In addition to positive and negative
feedback, however, one must also distinguish between first-
order and second-order feedback.

First-order feedback is almost mechanical in its opera-
tion. In a first-order situation, an organism's senses receive
information that indicate whether it is achieving its purpose.
Thus if a heating system is designed to keep the room temperature between seventy and seventy-four degrees, the unit
can turn on only if the temperature is below seventy and stop
only if the temperature is above seventy-four. It cannot keep
the temperature at sixty-eight unless it is readjusted or has
broken down. It cannot control its goal, it can seek only to
maintain it.

Second-order feedback requires a much more sophisticated information net than first-order feedback requires. In
order for a system to have second-order capabilities, it must
have information about the external realm, information
about itself or the state of the organism, and a memory of
past events. Only human systems are capable of second-order
feedback, which indicates a reordering of first-order purposes

and may lead to a greater achievement of these purposes. Only in human systems can we change the goals we seek. Without these second-order attributes, the organism in question cannot be autonomous, and without autonomy the organism cannot have second-order potential. As Deutsch describes it:

> A first order purpose in a feedback net would be the seeking of immediate satisfaction. . . . By a second order purpose would be meant that the internal and external state of the net that would seem to offer . . . the largest probability of the net's continued ability to seek first order purposes.[72]
>
> . . . autonomy in the long run depends on memory. Where all memory is lost, where all past information and preferences have ceased to be effective, we are no longer dealing with a self-determining individual or social group, but with a self-steering automaton. . . . A society or community that is to steer itself must continue to receive a full flow of information: First information about the world outside; second, information about the past; . . . and third, information about itself and its own parts.[73]

It is this characteristic of human systems that makes goal changes possible. To the degree that different individuals have different memories and different information flows, the intensity and direction of second-order changes are likely to differ. Even if given individuals have the same current information flows but have different memories, their behavior is likely to differ.

All organisms have within themselves additional units that may be important for explaining individual differences; that is, they have sensory units that receive information flows. Within these sensory units, "filters" separate real information from "static" or "noise." In human systems, the filters are constructed or changed by the interaction of current and past information. The individual selects and abstracts in order to cope with incoming information flows.[74]

If selection and abstraction are processes connected with memory, then the very process by which new information is allowed into the organism is subject to individual difference. This is extremely important in both first-order and second-order feedback. If an individual has so constructed his filters as to filter out all information save positive feedback, no change can take place. The degree to which negative feedback is allowed into the organism thus becomes central to the question of flexibility of foreign policy leaders.

As we have seen, Deutsch considers memory an important factor in decision making and foreign policy. Other scholars—not considered communication theorists—agree, for example, Morgenthau (lessons from history),[75] Allison (understanding by analogy),[76] Paige (information drawn from the past),[77] de Rivera (a constant to reduce uncertainty),[78] Greenstein (propositions 1,8,11),[79] and Snyder (adult socialization).[80] The problem is that although they all believe that individual memory is important, they have done little empirical investigation of the subject.

There are several reasons for this anomalous situation. It may be simply too difficult and too time-consuming to study memory. It may be all but impossible to do a psychobiography of all major leaders, one that could give a perfect picture of the events that make up their memory. Second, memory, regardless of its analytical utility, may be impossible to operationalize in a meaningful fashion. Third, memory may be too broad a concept to be useful and may have to be segmented before it can be researched.

This last point is important. Although we can speak of general memory, we can also view memory as composed of many distinct elements. Holsti suggests that we can view memory as "the belief system composed of a number of 'Images' of past, present, and future, includ[ing] 'all the accumulated, organized knowledge that the organism has about itself and the world.' "[81] Deutsch himself recognized that memory could be composed of different elements. In his model, "A Functional Diagram of Information Flow in Foreign Policy Decisions,"[82] he listed as discrete elements: deeply stored memory, current memory, selective memory, and selective recall. This multifaceted concept of memory will be adopted here for our study of flexibility in foreign policy.[83]

A Framework of Flexible Foreign Policy Behavior

Political science, like astronomy, cannot rely on laboratory experiments to test theories. Since it is difficult to obtain a leader's cooperation and consent to submit to an experiment under controlled conditions, we must instead test our theories by constructing a framework in which as many elements as possible can be held constant and in which any bias that exists will not skew our results.

Such a framework must rest on a definition of memory that includes the concepts of referents, goal theme, and policy theme. A major contention here is that the relationship among these concepts can be employed to determine the likelihood of flexible behavior on the part of any decision-maker, since the three concepts related to memory have been directly related to the perceptions of decision-makers. We have assumed that differences in perception will lead to differences in behavior. Another point arises here. I have suggested that feedback is instrumental in changing behavior and that negative or corrective feedback, if perceived, is likely to lead to behavior change: if the organism perceives that its prior acts are not beneficial, it will change its behavior.[84] In addition, if the organism is human and is faced with a high degree of negative feedback, second-order change would be possible. I also suggested that the perceptual filters of the individual allow only certain types of information to enter the organism; the condition of the filters, therefore, is very important. If an individual's perceptual filters admit only positive feedback, then no amount of negative feedback in the environment is likely to change behavior.

One way to approach this problem is to determine an objective situation in which a large amount of negative feedback is being directed at the organism, specifically, situations in which each decision-maker has experienced a large amount of negative feedback. Then an examination of his behavior will reveal whether he has demonstrated any flexibility from former behaviors in foreign policy. A crisis meets these requirements. In crisis, large amounts of feedback are received. Moreover, in crises that are deemed failures, feedback is negative.[85] If a leader exhibits any flexible behavior, he should therefore do so after he has failed in a crisis.

Moreover, crisis situations by definition contain other elements essential to the type of research that is being suggested. First, leadership and individual-level variables are likely to be important in crisis situations. Second, a leader's mental set (intellectual baggage) is likely to be important in crisis situations. Third, crisis situations, because of high threat, are likely to involve core values of some type. Fourth, the information channels during a crisis are operating at extremely high levels, thus increasing the probability that the individuals involved will be receiving many feedback cues leading to a high degree of ambiguity and the necessity of somehow reorganizing the incoming information.

A decision-maker's perception of negative feedback should lead to either a change in policy (actions to be taken) or a change in goals (change in the desired future state). The nature of the perception, however, and the reaction to this perception can vary. Some decision-makers may react to negative feedback by increasing the resources committed to an activity without any examination of goals. The Vietnam war is often viewed in this light. Other decision-makers may react to negative feedback by assuming that some other actor has taken an action merely to mislead them. Dulles seems to have held this opinion about the Soviet Union. These examples indicate some type of reaction to negative feedback, but the degree of flexibility they illustrate is questionable.

To the degree that an individual does not change after he has received a large input of negative feedback, we would assume that his perceptual screens are constructed either to discount or to eliminate the negative feedback. The condition of the perceptual screens, therefore, ought to be highly related to the degree of change exhibited by the individual.

As noted, the state of the perceptual filters—their construction, maintenance, and change—are related to memory.[86] The memory itself serves as part of the filters. These filters in turn have many functions, among the most important of which is selecting out unneeded information, or "static." They can be changed when memory combines with new information to reorder goals. Viewed in this manner, memory becomes important to any model of flexibility.

The problem with memory, however, is that it may be too broad to be analytically useful. For our purposes, therefore, memory will be divided into several component parts. At the most general level, memory consists of two major elements, which will be labeled *referents* and *themes. Referents* are the cognitive *objects* used by a leader, of which events form a significant part. They are characterized by several significant dimensions. The first is a temporal dimension. Thus, referents can be divided into past, present, and future referents: past referents are objects or events that existed before the period to be examined; present referents are those existing during the period to be examined; future referents are those perceived as likely to occur after the period to be examined. A second important dimension is spacial. Referents can be domestic or foreign. Domestic referents are objects or events internal to the United States. Foreign referents are objects or events outside the United States. A third dimension is that of affect. Referents are either positive or negative. A positive referent is one that is looked upon favorably; a negative referent, in contrast, is looked upon unfavorably.

The second element associated with memory is that of theme. (Theme may be more a product of memory than memory itself. However, that distinction, if it exists, is not relevant to the problem at hand.) *Theme* is defined as the lessons or attitudes that a leader associates with or attributes to a referent. Theme itself can be subdivided into: goal and policy themes. *Goal theme* refers to the future state that the decision-maker desires, the "what" of foreign policy. As such, a goal theme also incorporates the values that a decision-maker holds. *Policy theme,* therefore, becomes the "how."

Thus, a research design based on these concepts can be established so that several requirements are met: control for situation so that negative feedback is present; control for role, by investigating only presidents and secretaries of state; and control for differences in data, by using the same type of data sources for all the individuals in the study.

This framework contains independent, intervening, and dependent variables. The independent variables can be described as the "intellectual baggage" that a decision-maker brings to a crisis. This baggage describes the referents and themes employed by a decision-maker before a crisis. The intervening variables are crisis and failure. In order for a case to be included in this study, both intervening variables must be present. The dependent variables can be termed the "intellectual baggage" a decision-maker takes with him after a crisis.

As mentioned earlier, we are interested in degrees of flexibility. We must therefore have some idea of how flexibility can be scaled. The following method will be used to determine the degree of flexibility. If a leader exhibits change in both goal and policy themes, this will be considered the most significant change, regardless of referent. Change in both goals and policies is indicative of both first-order and second-order feedback. The next most significant change will be a change in goal but no change in referent and policy. In this case, second-order feedback is again present. The third most significant will be change in policy theme but no change in goal and referent. This would indicate the presence of first-order feedback. The least significant would be change in referent but no change in goal and policy. In this case, the subject is probably engaging in rhetoric, merely changing his examples and allusions to win a particular audience. This is very similar to the techniques lawyers use in their statements to juries. At the extreme, this type of change can even be considered rationalization.

As for policy theme itself, change within that category indicates a type of perceptual filter that should be examined. This type of filter usually leads to an assessment indicating that the goals the leader is pursuing are correct (and that even the policies themselves are aimed in the proper direction) but that the failure was one of degree rather than kind. This assessment is usually followed by an intensification of the initial, unsuccessful behavior.

In order to measure change, we must have a base line from which to mark change. Therefore our independent variable will be determined for a period of time before the onset of a crisis that is deemed a failure. The statements and speeches of the selected leaders will be coded for referent and themes, and scores for these variables will be recorded. This information will then serve as a base line against which the dependent variables—behavior after crisis failure—can be compared. The intervening variable will be constructed so that all the crisis failures meet a minimum standard of comparability.

Hypotheses

Having described the framework, I must now turn to some of the hypotheses that it generates. Several major questions arise from the literature and the framework. The most basic is: do leaders exhibit flexible foreign policy behavior? This, of course, is not a hypothesis. However, we can gain insight into this problem by examining the following hypothesis: if leaders receive large amounts of negative feedback, they will change their foreign policy behavior. The null hypothesis could also be examined: there is no relationship between change in foreign policy behavior and amount of negative feedback received. These two hypotheses represent the two extremes in behavior. For example, John Foster Dulles seemed to exhibit little or no flexibility, as Holsti concludes:

> These findings have somewhat sobering implications. . . . They suggest the fallacy of thinking that peaceful settlements of outstanding international issues is simply a problem of devising good plans. Clearly as long as decision-makers on either side of the Cold War adhere to rigid images of the other party there is little likelihood that even genuine bids to decrease tensions will have the desired effect. . . . To the extent that each side undeviatingly interprets new information, even friendly bids, in a manner calculated to preserve the original image [memory screen] the two nation system is a closed one.[87]

The basis for the first general hypothesis is the relationship between a decision-maker's view of the situation and the crisis itself. The greater the congruence between referents and the current situation, the greater the likelihood of change. There may be several reasons for this relationship. The most obvious one is that the decision-maker who chooses referents that are congruent to the situation at hand—in terms of geographical region, type of issue, degree of involvement, and so forth—is likely to have a greater knowledge of the area and is therefore likely to be able to sort out the most important information. The first general hypothesis can be stated as follows:

I. The greater the congruence between referents and the current situation, the greater the flexibility that will be exhibited.

This general hypothesis can be divided into a number of more specific hypotheses:

I-1. Leaders who use more past domestic referents will tend to be less flexible.

I-2. Leaders who use more past foreign referents will be only slightly more flexible than leaders who use past domestic referents.

I-3. Leaders who use more present domestic referents will tend to show no consistent pattern of flexible behavior.

I-4. Leaders who use more present foreign referents will tend to be the most flexible.

I-5. Leaders who use more future domestic referents will tend to have no consistent pattern of flexible behavior.

I-6. Leaders who use more future foreign referents will tend to be slightly less flexible than leaders who use more present foreign referents.

Another relationship the framework suggests is that between referent and goal. Again, the concept of congruence is necessary for an understanding of this hypothesis. By *congruence* I mean the degree of similarity, in this case, between referent and goal theme. This hypothesis, which links two aspects of memory with flexibility, in a sense addresses the question of choice of perceptual filters. Simply stated, it is,

II. The greater the congruence between referents and goal theme in terms of issue, the greater the flexibility that will be exhibited.

Thus, if a leader was concerned with the economic boycott of an African nation and was using referents of past military invasions of Europe, we would expect him to exhibit little or no flexible behavior. This inflexibility would be due in part to the fact that the filter chosen was not precise enough to handle the information flow from the current situation.

This general hypothesis leads to several more specific hypotheses based on congruence. In communications, the more sophisticated the filter, the greater the likelihood that the information reaching the organism will be assessed and acted upon swiftly and with precision. In terms of congruence, the state of the filters can have the following attributes: geographical, foreign-domestic, temporal, United States involvement, policy type, and issue. Geographical congruence refers to whether the referent and goal in terms of issue occurred in the same geographical region. Foreign-domestic refers to whether the events took place within the United States or abroad. Temporal refers to whether the events in question took place in the past, present, or future. United States involvement is defined as whether the United States government was a direct participant in the actions in question. Policy could be military, economic, diplomatic, and so forth. Finally, issue is defined as the "subject matter" of a particular series of events. The hypotheses listed below are not exclusive; rather, each one refers to a specific type of congruence.

II-1. The greater the congruence between referent and goal regionally, the greater the flexible behavior.

II-2. The greater the congruence between referent and goal in terms of foreign-domestic concerns, the greater the flexible behavior.

II-3. The greater the congruence between referent and goal temporally, the greater the flexible behavior.

II-4. The greater the congruence between referent and goal in terms of United States involvement, the greater the flexible behavior.

II-5. The greater the congruence between referent and goal in terms of policy type, the greater the flexible behavior.

II-6. The greater the congruence between referent and goal in terms of issue, the greater the flexible behavior.

Another set of hypotheses relates to the null hypothesis, which can be stated as follows:

III.   There is no relationship between foreign policy be-
       havior and the presence of negative feedback.

This hypothesis is included because it has been argued that decision-makers pay little or no attention to current situations and that they are all basically closed-minded. The general hypothesis leads to several more specific hypotheses.

III-1. There will be no significant difference between
       foreign policy referents before and after a crisis.
III-2. There will be no significant difference between
       foreign policy goal themes before and after a crisis.
III-3. There will be no significant difference between
       foreign policy policy themes before and after a
       crisis.

A final general hypothesis is based upon the premise that negative feedback can be highly compartmentalized. Thus, even though a leader may not seem to have changed his general goals and policy, he may have changed dramatically in those areas related to the crisis. Therefore, we can state the general hypothesis as follows:

IV.   A decision-maker will exhibit flexible behavior in
      areas that are similar to the substance of the crisis
      he has just experienced.

This general hypothesis can be viewed in terms of a number of more specific hypotheses.

IV-1. Leaders will exhibit flexible behavior in those areas
      that are most congruent with the substance of crisis
      in terms of region, issue, and policy type.

IV-2. Leaders will exhibit little or no flexible behavior
in those areas that are not congruent with the substance of the crisis in terms of region, issue, and
policy type.

IV-3. Leaders will exhibit no discernible pattern of flexible behavior in those areas that are congruent with
the substance of a crisis in terms of only *one* of the
following: region, issue, policy type.

As indicated, we are concerned primarily with decision-
makers in the foreign policy area that might have an impact
on crisis decisions and on foreign policy in general. I have
chosen the postwar presidents and secretaries of state because
they meet the requirements that have been established. Moreover, by choosing pairs of individuals rather than single individuals, we have an additional basis for comparison. In the
following chapter, I discuss in detail the research design and
the justification for the research decisions in terms of variables to be examined, selection of the number of cases, data
sources, and the methods employed for analyzing the data.

A Model for Predicting Behavior: Research Design and Crisis Measurement Techniques

In order to research the insights found in Chapter 2, several problems must be overcome. These include information sources, operationalization of the variables, and the choice of manipulative techniques that will be appropriate to the data collected. In addition, for a framework of analysis to have real value, the hypotheses it generates must be testable. This chapter investigates the ways in which some of the concepts discussed in Chapter 2 can be operationalized and measured. Data sources are also suggested, and the ways in which those sources can be used to test hypotheses are presented.

The Data Sources and Comparability across Cases

Public Documents

The data used in this study come primarily from public documents, which include speeches, transcripts of news conferences, and testimony before congressional committees. This data source will be used for the independent and dependent variables. The use of public documents, however, raises questions of validity and reliability. As for validity, the basic question is whether public documents measure the types of perceptual variables that we are interested in examining. In short are they valid data sources? Abraham Kaplan describes and defines validity as follows:

> The root meaning of the word "validity" is the same as that of the word "value:" both derive from a term meaning strength. The validity of a measurement consists in what it is able to accomplish, or more accurately, in what *we* are able to do with it. Plainly this "what" depends on the context of the measurement's use. . . . The usual characterization of a valid measurement is that it is one which "measures what it purports to measure." Whether it does so is in turn established in two fundamentally different ways, though which is relevant may vary from case to case, and the distinction is seldom a sharp one even for a single context. Briefly, one is a matter of definition, the other of empirical connections.[1]

According to this definition, public documents are usually considered a quite acceptable source, and they have been used in studies that examine similar types of questions. Since this study centers upon an individual decision-maker's perceptions of an event or series of events, the question is whether public documents are accurate or "valid" representations of the individual's perceptions or whether they logically correspond to the statesman's beliefs.

Other researchers who are interested in the same type of variables have used public documents for their data source and have tested their data for validity. Ole Holsti, for example, used public documents to investigate the belief system of John Foster Dulles. In order to check the validity of his data, he communicated with several of Dulles's close associates and found that Dulles's public statements and private beliefs were highly correlated.[2] Several other authors have also found that public statements tend to reflect the private beliefs of the individuals who make the statements. For example, Gutierrez found this true for Rusk, and McLellan for Acheson.[3] It should be noted that these three authors deal with individuals who will appear in our study also.

In addition to the argument that similar studies have used validity tests for public documents, the contention that public documents are valid sources is further supported by the employment of additional tests of validity. Extensive biographical materials are used to see whether the decision-maker's public statements correspond in general to his attitudes and beliefs as assessed by his biographers and former associates.

However, the use of public documents as a data source incurs several additional problems. Apart from such questions as whether leaders intentionally mislead the public, we have the serious difficulty of leaders who lie consistently over the entire period of the study. Although the validity tests cited earlier may mitigate this problem, the possibility that a decision-maker lies consistently over a long period of time is indeed a grave problem, even if it is only an unlikely possibility. News conferences and congressional hearings serve as a check on the truth of certain statements made by the president and the secretary of state. If the president or the secretary of state lies, his claim will quite likely be challenged by the questioners—either in a news conference in the case of the president or in a congressional hearing in the case of the secretary of state. Both formats allow inquiries about inconsistencies between present and previous statements and between present and previous actions.

If a leader lies constantly during the entire time period of the study, a serious problem does exist. Although the probability that a leader will be able to mislead the public for so long a time before and after a crisis is quite small, that possibility must be taken into account. If consistent lying is suspected, the academic literature will tend to indicate whether the suspected misstatements did in fact occur. Although this type of check does not solve the problem completely, it does indicate that some method can be found to check the veracity of a leader's statements.

Another serious problem in the use of public documents

is the possibility of obtaining an unrepresentative (skewed) sample. Logically, public statements and documents will probably tend to be skewed toward consistency. It is, after all, more difficult to back away from a position or statements taken or made in public than positions or statements taken or made in private. But although at first glance this skewing seems to be a disadvantage (since the purpose of the research is to examine change), any results that indicate change in a sample skewed toward consistency would seem to make the results even more significant.

It should be noted that public documents are also considered foreign policy events. Any public statement, speech, or news conference usually appears in the media, reported as occurrences or events. Public documents and events therefore have rather similar advantages and disadvantages; they have numerous uses for the study of foreign policy.

In addition to perceptual studies, the behavior of elite groups in certain situations has been investigated using public documents as a data source.[4] Event data have also been employed to measure systematically the interaction of "foreign policy" events between nations or the impact of one actor or group of actors upon another actor or group of actors. Such studies have been undertaken by projects such as *World Events/Interaction Survey (WEIS), Comparative Research on the Events of Nations (CREON)*, the *Nonstate Actor Project (NOSTAC)*, and the *Multiple Issue Systems Event Research Project (MISER)*. Although the results of these projects have varied widely, the event data approach, which Hermann classifies as "microanalytic," has been associated with some of the major advances in international political research in recent years.[5]

By using publicly available documents for all the individuals under study, we also avoid the problem of comparability across cases. The sources of data will be the same for all individuals, and thus the question of their comparability need not concern us. Other questions of comparability should be mentioned. It may prove rather difficult to compare two decision-makers if one of them makes only one public statement during the time period under study and the second makes many public statements. This situation is unlikely to occur, but if the data indicate that a spread of this nature exists, it will be necessary to drop a particular case from the study.

It is not possible to solve all the problems inherent in the use of public documents. (Indeed, no data source will be completely without disadvantages.) However, in terms of reliability, comparability, and validity,[6] public documents seem to have more advantages than disadvantages for the independent and dependent variables and therefore will be employed in this study.

Event Data

The intervening variables in this study are foreign policy crises and failures. In selecting data sources to examine for both crises and failures, we must exercise a good deal of caution so as to ensure that the determination of both crisis and failure is objective and comparable across cases.

Our definition of crisis involves three dimensions: time, surprise, and threat.[7] Since this method of measuring crisis is adapted from Thomas L. Brewer, it may be useful to examine the data sources he used for his research, namely, the *New York Times Index.*[8] Brewer himself admits that "such data— which may be regarded as a variant form of 'events' data— must of course be evaluated in terms of several validity and reliability criteria."[9] And since this study uses the same source, a discussion of the validity of the data source itself seems appropriate. It should be remembered that since crisis, in the sense in which it is here empoyed, involves foreign actors as well as the United States and, moreover, involves issues of high salience, a data source must not tend to over-bias its reportage toward foreign coverage or overreport violent actions.

Most criticisms of event data can actually be viewed as criticisms of the *New York Times,* yet adherence to a single high-quality source, especially for crises in which the United States is involved, seems to be the best way of assuming either randomness of error or consistency of bias, no matter what the editorial position or idiosyncrasies of reportage are at any given time. Charles McClelland argues in favor of coding the *New York Times* in the following manner:

> The question of whose coding system matches correctly to reality is virtually unanswerable. When everybody has a bias, what test could there be for objectivity? . . . The solution that is available is to set aside the problem of unbiased truth and to analyze over time the reports that pass through *one* bias-filter of a national press. The best choice that can be made of a single source is the *New York Times.* This paper must be assumed to filter the news with an American bias but it is an exceptionally rich source of international political events.[10]

In addition, since we are dealing with events that are, by definition, of great interest to an American audience, even the criticism of "national bias" becomes somewhat moot. And there are several other reasons for employment of the *New York Times* as a data source. As Stephen Salmore suggests:

> McClelland selected the *New York Times* as his sole data source for a number of reasons. Many scholars and statesmen consider it a document of historical record. It is readily available and promises to continue to be so in the future, thereby offering some assurances of continuity. The newspaper makes a conscious attempt to be comprehensive and thorough in its coverage, and indeed interprets its role as an official recorder of world events. Because of this conscious orientation, it is not unreasonable for the researcher to assume that in preparing the

paper, the criteria used for inclusion of articles and their amount of elaboration will remain fairly constant over time.[11]

Many questions could be raised concerning inclusion rules used by the *Times.* The most important question from the standpoint of determining crisis is: Does the data source tend to report certain types of behavior more intensively than others? Stated differently this question becomes, Does the *Times* tend to overreport conflictful actions? In order to address this concern, we must first examine the role of the *New York Times* itself:

> In each major power one newspaper stands out as an organ of elite opinion. Usually semiofficial, always intimate with the government, these "prestige papers" are read by public officials, journalists, scholars, and business leaders. They are read not only in their own countries, but also abroad by those whose business it is to keep track of world affairs. . . . We find, then, that despite local and individual variations, the prestige paper has come to be an important and respected institution. Governments, politicians, and businessmen depend upon it. One might ask what would happen in Washington if the *New York Times* stopped publication and no other paper took its place.[12]

The *Times* has been shown to be an important source of information for State Department bureaucracy.[13] It is also an important element of the "milieu" in which a United States decision-maker operates.[14] As such, it is an example of what James N. Rosenau has called "quality" media.[15] Rosenau suggests that quality media are less prone to overreport conflictful activity. The popular media, in contrast, tend to be less sensitive to the background of situations until situations become sufficiently attention-getting, "at which point they would circulate sensational and oversimplified headlines. On the other hand, the quality media would sustain a continuous flow of considered opinion."[16]

In short, the validity of the *New York Times Index* as a
data source for coding purposes (i.e., the assigning of numeri-
cal values to certain statements and concepts) for variables
related to crisis has been demonstrated by analogy to the
New York Times itself. The index is merely an abbreviated
listing of the same types of information one would obtain if
one coded the *Times* itself. Again, Brewer's work on the
validity of the *New York Times Index* is most enlightening:

> The validity of any given data set is the degree to which it does
> indeed measure what it is purported to measure. Three types
> are commonly distinguished: predictive [or criterion], content
> [or face], and construct. The data of the present study have
> been found to have predictive validity by two sets of tests. . . .
> One can argue and adduce evidence that the data also have
> content validity. The argument is based largely on the obser-
> vation that the American policy process . . . tends to be rather
> open and public and that therefore the *New York Times* con-
> stitutes a defensible data source. . . . The data have also been
> found to have construct validity inasmuch as the variables
> within each of the clusters . . . positively intercorrelate.[17]

Once the data source for crisis determination is established, it is necessary to establish the data source for failure.
As noted earlier, failure will be defined in terms of negative
feedback. A subjective measure of failure cannot be used,
since the ability of a decision-maker to react to perceived
negative feedback is one of the central concerns of this study.
We must find a data source, therefore, that can be used as an
objective measure of the amount of negative feedback present across cases.

The data source for the determination of failure will be
newspaper editorials during the crisis in question. These have
been chosen for a number of reasons. First, since newspapers
react to events much more quickly than scholarly journals
do, there is no problem of time lag. As indicated in our
earlier arguments about the role of newspapers such as the

New York Times, the news media also play such an important part in the "milieu" of decision-makers that if they agree
that a failure has occurred, there will be significant negative
feedback into the decision-making process.

The methods that will be employed to code and analyze
the various data sources will be discussed in the following sections. Each set of variables will be discussed separately, and
measurement techniques for each set of variables will be discussed immediately after the operational definitions have
been established.

The Independent Variables

The independent variables in this research will be the referents and themes used by leaders for a period of six months
before the onset of a crisis that has been deemed a failure.[18]
They are, in short, the "intellectual baggage" that a decision-
maker brings with him to a crisis. These variables are composed of elements of memory;[19] memory will here be operationalized in a new formulation, which borrows from many
foreign policy studies but has not been adapted directly from
any particular one. The use of referent and theme, for example, draws upon the general approach used by Karl
Deutsch.[20] The concept of memory is also informed by the
work of Holsti and his notion of "images."[21] Additional
refinements of the concepts of referent and theme owe much
to the work of authors such as Snyder,[22] Greenstein,[23]
Allison,[24] Paige,[25] de Rivera,[26] and even Morgenthau.[27]

A series of operationalizations and measurement techniques has been developed to assess the differences in the
theme and referents that a decision-maker could use. The
first variable we will discuss is *referent*—a cognitive object
cited by a leader. These cognitive objects, of which events
form a significant part, are divided into past, present, or future referents: past referents are those that have occurred or
existed before the first date of the sample period, present
referents are those occurring during the sample period, and

future referents are those that the decision-maker views as likely to occur. Referents will also be coded as to whether they are foreign or domestic: foreign policy referents are those that involve actors or targets outside the United States, domestic policy referents are those primarily involving actors and targets within the United States. Finally, referents will be coded for affect. A positive referent is a particular leader's judgment that the example used was a good precedent and should be repeated. A negative referent is defined as a bad precedent, which should *not* be repeated. Whether a referent is positive or negative will be determined by reference to the statements of the individual under study. Thus, if president X believes that the Japanese bombing of Pearl Harbor was a "good thing" and a precedent that should be repeated, then that past foreign referent must be considered positive. It may not be possible to code every referent for affect, but, wherever possible, this will be done.

In the most general sense, referents can be considered to be all the nouns contained within a particular section of a document. Examples of this coding method may indicate with greater clarity the type of coding procedures that will be employed.

> We have on numerous occasions demonstrated our willingness to come to the aid of others who are themselves threatened— both where we have treaty obligations and where, as in Greece or in Korea, we had no obligations.[28]

The mention of Greece and Korea will both be viewed as *past foreign referents*—these referents occurred in the past and were foreign.

> A primary purpose of this meeting of the Council of Ministers is to determine. . . .[29]

The OAS Council of Ministers meeting to which Rusk refers here is a *present foreign referent;* it occurred at the time Rusk was speaking. In all the examples used to illustrate the coding scheme, it should be remembered that the speeches used are not taken from any particular time period under study. Thus, by using a present referent for purposes of example, a referent occurring on the same day that the speech was made has been employed.

> We cannot imagine the survival of our own free institutions if areas of the world distant from our shores are to be subjugated by force or penetration.[30]

This statement contains two referents. The first—"survival of our own free institutions"—refers to the future conditions of American institutions and will thus be coded as a *future domestic referent*. The second—"areas of the world . . . are to be subjugated"—will be coded as a *future foreign referent*.

Similar illustrations can be provided for each type of referent. However, we have not yet offered examples of positive and negative referents. The final referent mentioned in our examples can illustrate a negative referent that is also future in orientation. The statement, "we cannot imagine . . . survival," can be coded as negative—because the decision-maker is indicating that this referent is undesirable and that one should *not* seek to achieve it.

Once all the referents have been coded for a given speech and all other documents during the sample period have been collected, several types of data manipulation will be performed. Raw scores per unit (speech, answer, and so forth)[31] and scores as a percentage of total referents will be computed for each unit. In addition, raw scores as a percentage of total referents will be calculated for the period as a whole. These measurement techniques will allow the following determinations to be made: first, the major referent type used in each unit; second, the prevalence of a type of referent as a percentage; third, the overall rankings of appearance in raw scores and percentages for the entire period.

Thus, we have a measure of appearance as well as a comparative frequency measure. The prevalence scale assumes that the higher the number of a certain type of referent, the higher the probability that this type of referent is relevant to a particular leader.

Given the measurements and manipulations suggested, rank-order correlation is also possible. All these measures together allow us to describe not only which referent was the most important in each unit but also which type of referent was the most important overall. By use of the four separate measures, we are able to determine whether any change has occurred within the given time period as well as across time periods.

The coding of referents allows us to test the hypotheses that relate the types of referents to the degree of flexible behavior.[32] All the hypotheses that relate referent to behavior change are phrased as "the more . . . the less" or as "the more . . . the more." By employing different measurement techniques, we have several scales for "the more"; and several tests of each hypothesis, both in terms of single individuals and in terms of comparisons among individuals in the study, are possible.

Our next task is to define and operationalize the variable we call "goal theme." *Goal theme* is defined as the future state that the decision-maker desires, the "what" of foreign policy.[33] These desired future states or goal themes must be mentioned by the leader in question in order to be considered codable. Goal theme will be coded for the same universe of documents as referents. The coding system will rely on paragraph thematic analysis. This should determine the particular goal of each section or paragraph of a unit being coded. This coding method is judgmental, but in order to control as much as possible for differing perceptions on the part of the coder, the coding method requires that the information upon which the judgment is made be entered *verbatim* on the coding sheets.

As nouns can be considered referents, verbs or conditional clauses will reveal much about goal themes. For example, in the clause, "in order to provide security in the Pacific Basin, I am sending one million men to Hawaii," the statement about security is obviously the goal theme. The coder must list the complete phrase, thus allowing for collapsing or typologizing of action categories.

Several of our hypotheses involve the congruence between referent and goal theme.[34] These hypotheses are designed to examine the relationship of differing degrees of congruence with flexible behavior. In order to test these hypotheses, we must create a measure of congruence. This is done by establishing a sixfold scoring system that allows us to measure the congruence between referent and goal theme. Congruence is defined as an exact match for each of six variables in the scoring system. The score will be calculated by the following formula:

$$\frac{\text{number of exact matches}}{6} = \text{congruence score from 0.0 to 1.00.}$$

The six variables in the scoring system are:

1. *Regional:* do the referent and theme involve the same geographical area?
2. *Foreign-Domestic:* do the referent and goal theme involve either domestic or foreign concerns?
3. *Temporal:* do referents and goal theme agree in terms of past, present, and future?
4. *United States Involvement:* was the United States a participant in the referent used and in the issue at hand?
5. *Policy Type:* what type of policy is associated with the referent: military, economic, diplomatic?
6. *Issue:* do the referent and goal theme refer to the same general subject? For example, are they both concerned with security or the spread of communism?

An example may indicate how the coding scheme operates.

We shall return to a troubled world . . . to such matters as
Berlin, Laos, Vietnam, the Congo . . . where the struggle to
maintain principles of independence and human freedom goes
forward. . . . The friends of freedom must stand together. . . .
And we see, as others have seen at this meeting, a Cuba re-
leased from its nightmare.[35]

In terms of data collection, congruence scores would be
calculated for each of the referents listed—Berlin, Laos, Vietnam, and the Congo. Each referent is scored vis-à-vis the goal
theme, and the scores are averaged to determine a mean score
for the particular unit in question. As an illustration, we will
code only the Congo referent, examining each variable for
exact matches and then computing the congruence score.

1. *Regional:* no congruence—referent outside Latin
   America
2. *Foreign-Domestic:* congruent—both foreign
3. *Temporal:* congruent—both refer to ongoing situations
4. *United States Involvement:* no congruence—United
   States directly involved in Cuba and not directly involved in Congo
5. *Policy Type:* no congruence—Cuba involved economic
   boycott; Congo involved United Nations peacekeeping
   force
6. *Issue:* congruent—according to Mr. Rusk, both situations involve "struggles for human freedom."

The score for congruence is thus 0.50. It should be obvious that this score will not be directly obtainable for all units
coded. If it is impossible to determine congruence for a specific variable, that variable will be considered noncongruent. If
no information is available about a particular goal theme,
then that goal theme will be regarded as missing data.

After each unit has been coded for congruence, we can
determine the mean score for each unit and the mean congruence score for the period as a whole. It should be noted

that in calculating the mean congruence score for the whole period, individual congruence scores, rather than the mean scores, will be averaged for each unit coded.

Congruence scores allow us to determine whether the leader in question had high or low scores for different issues, whether the congruence scores increase or decrease over each period, or whether these scores remain stable or change dramatically over the two periods under study. They also allow us to plot a congruence line for each period in question so that if change is incremental rather than related to the intervening variables (crisis failure), that can be shown. This type of analysis serves as an additional test of our hypotheses about the relationship of congruence to flexible behavior.

The last major independent variable is policy theme. *Policy theme* is the means employed or advocated by a decision-maker in pursuit of the goal theme. Thus, it is the "how" of foreign policy. A coding scheme for policy theme must be able to identify, in public documents, actions or proposed actions that deal with foreign policy. Logically, these actions or proposed actions may vary from extremely belligerent to extremely conciliatory. What is needed is a coding system that allows for this great variability.

Some coding systems have been devised to handle actions within a broad range. Although the purposes differ, the coding system used in *The World Events Interaction Survey (WEIS)* can be adapted to our research.[36] The *WEIS* project used a twenty-two-category system for coding events.[37] This system can be employed usefully in the coding of public documents, including, but not limited to, news items.

This coding scheme allows us to code the key policy themes precisely; at the same time, the collapsed categories enable us to make more general comparisons. The initial coding of policy themes will be based directly on the twenty-two-category *WEIS* system; but if the data require it (as indicated by a large number of empty cells), they can be collapsed into five more general categories. This collapsing is based upon the *WEIS* system, except that both "offensive" and "defensive verbal conflict" are included in a category called "verbal conflict."[38]

Several steps are based on this coding scheme. First, frequency scores for the entire period will be calculated. Second, a weighted measure of policy themes will be calculated for each unit and for the period as a whole. The weighted measure will be calculated in the following manner. Cooperative policy deeds will be given a weight of +3. The 3 weight indicates that deeds imply greater commitment than words, and the plus sign indicates support for the system as it then exists. Cooperative verbal behavior will be assigned a weight of +2. The plus sign again indicates support for the status quo, and the value 2 indicates that verbal behavior implies less commitment than deeds. Participant policy themes will be assigned a weight of +1. Conflictful verbal behavior is assigned a weight of –2. Finally, conflictful deed behavior will be assigned a weight of –3.

After assigning weights to all the policy themes in a unit, one can either count the appearance of each type of policy theme or calculate a weighted average of policy themes based on the following formula:

cooperative policy theme deed = (COPTD)
cooperative policy theme word = (COPTW)
participant policy theme = (PPT)
conflictful policy theme word = (CPTW)
conflictful policy theme deed = (CPTD)

$$\frac{3(COPTD) + 2(COPTW) + PPT - 2(CPTW) - 3(CPTD)}{N} = \text{weighted average of policy themes}$$

This formula indicates what type of policy theme was most important in a given unit on a weighted basis. Thus for each unit, a determination of the most frequent type of policy theme can be made. At the same time, by employing the weighted average a determination can be made whether the most frequent type of policy theme is also the one with the greatest salience or weight.

For example, a major foreign policy address made by a president contains 4 COPTD, 10 COPTW, 2 PPT, 6 CPTW, and 2 CPTD. Our frequency measure indicates that the prevalent policy theme in the speech is cooperative verbal policy themes. On the other hand, the weighted score would be computed as follows:

$$\frac{3(4) + 2(10) + 2 - 2(6) - 3(2)}{24} = 0.67.$$

Thus, the weighted score indicates that on balance the unit involved was much less dominated by cooperative words and was probably closer to participant activity.

Frequencies and weighted measures will also be determined for each unit and for the period as a whole, thus enabling us to have greater confidence that the samples are not skewed.

These measurements enable us to plot change within the periods as well as change between periods. We have constructed measures that will allow us to discover incremental change if it takes place, thereby enhancing our ability to determine the slope of change and to examine the "null" hypothesis, which states that crisis has no effect on the flexibility of foreign policy leaders.

The independent variables in this study will be measured for a period of six months before the onset of a crisis.[39] This time period is sufficient to determine the base line of referents and themes used by any given decision-maker. All the publicly available speeches, documents, and testimony will be included for coding purposes. All public documents related to foreign policy will be coded. In the case of news conferences, only questions or statements that refer to foreign policy will be coded. In the case of major addresses by the president, sections or paragraphs that relate to foreign policy will be coded (see Table 1).

TABLE 1

SAMPLE DATES FOR INDEPENDENT VARIABLES INCLUDING CRISIS DATES*

CASE	SAMPLE DATES		CRISIS DATES	
	First Date	Last Date	First Date	Last Date
Czechoslovakia	Aug. 19,1947	Feb. 19,1948	Feb. 20,1948	Feb. 25,1948
PRC Intervention in Korea	Apr. 13,1950	Oct. 13,1950	Oct. 14,1950	Nov. 14,1950
Hungary	May 31,1956	Oct. 31,1956	Nov. 1,1956	Nov. 4,1956
Lebanon	Jan. 13,1958	Jul. 13,1958	Jul. 14,1958	Aug. 3,1958
Berlin	Feb. 12,1961	Aug. 12,1961	Aug. 13,1961	Sep. 14,1961
Dominican Republic	Oct. 24,1964	Apr. 24,1965	Apr. 25,1965	Apr. 30,1965
Tet Offensive	Jul. 23,1967	Jan. 23,1968	Jan. 24,1968	Feb. 2,1968
Oct. Mid East War	Apr. 5,1973	Oct. 5,1973	Oct. 6,1973	Oct. 22,1973

*The crisis dates have been determined by reference to the academic literature and the New York Times Index. After determining the crisis dates sample dates for the independent variables were determined by counting backward six calender months beginning with the day prior to the onset of the crisis.

The Intervening Variables

Crisis

The first major intervening variable used in the research design is that of crisis. As already defined, a crisis is an event in which the elements of high threat, short time, and surprise come together in a particular situation.[40] The major difficulty with this definition, however, is the problem of operationalization. The concepts of high threat and surprise are difficult to quantify, and surprise may be so idiosyncratic that objective measures of surprise are not satisfactory. Difficulty in operationalization does not necessarily mean, however, that the concept itself is not useful.

Many researchers have sought to define crisis. Charles McClelland, for example, views crisis as an observable change in the intensity and frequency of interaction,[41] but Paige, Holsti, and Hermann tend to view the variables of crisis as more perceptual in character.[42] In short, the general definition of crisis varies with the individual researcher. Even if crisis is indeed composed of the three elements mentioned above, we are still faced with the rather difficult problem of developing measures for them. Some work, however, has been done in this area, and we will rely heavily upon it in order to operationalize crisis[43]; however, we will add to the conditions of crisis already stated the further requirement that for a crisis to be included in the study it must be "other-inspired." *Other-inspired* means that the crisis situation must have been originally initiated by actors outside the United States. This rule will avoid the possibility that a crisis was "planned" by a United States actor. It also avoids the complication of a United States–initiated action that turned into a crisis and then was deemed a failure. However, if the verification scheme does not allow this requirement to stand, then modifications will be made with an eye to making the intervening variables in each case as compatible as possible.

The list of possible crises is drawn from academic and

popular literature. These cases have a certain "face validity," but only by verification will we have confidence that they were indeed crises as we have defined crises. (It should be noted that the Bay of Pigs invasion has been omitted from the list in order to avoid the problem that the Bay of Pigs was United States–inspired.)

These crises (see Table 1) will be coded in a manner adapted from Thomas L. Brewer,[44] and the basic coding scheme will involve a determination of high threat, short time, and surprise. Only if an event scores high on all three variables will it be a crisis.

The degree of threat is in effect based on a notion of salience: the higher the salience of a given event, the higher the potential threat to the decision-makers in question. An event will be considered high-threat if the *New York Times Index* has at least three entries on that event for each day of the crisis. A minimum of ten index entries, in addition to the per day requirement, will be necessary to regard an event as high-threat.

In defining "short time," we will depend upon the complexity of the problem to be solved and "clock time" available for its solution. Support for this approach can be found in the work of Hermann,[45] Robinson,[46] and Robinson and Snyder.[47] "Clock time" is the amount of time in the conventional sense—days, weeks, etc.—that will elapse before the situation will significantly alter the circumstances under which a decision must be made. Clock time will be considered short if the situation changed after no more than one month.[48] The complexity of the problem is measured by the number of people involved, the number of tasks to be performed, and the like. Given the suggested list of possible crises, the complexity issue is true almost by definition.

Surprise will be operationalized in terms of the amount of precedent for the situation, in short, whether there was any advance notice that this particular situation might develop. Precedent is determined by examining the *New*

TABLE 2

SAMPLE DATES FOR DETERMINING SURPRISE

EVENT	SAMPLE DATES	
	First Date	Last Date
Czechoslovakia	Jan. 20	Feb. 13
PRC in Korea	Sep. 14	Oct. 7
Hungary	Oct. 1	Oct. 25
Lebanon	Jun. 14	Jul. 7
Berlin	Jul. 13	Aug. 6
Dominican Republic	Mar. 25	Apr. 18
Tet Offensive	Dec. 24	Jan. 17
Mid East War	Sep. 6	Sep. 29

York Times Index for a period of one month prior to the onset of the event in question. If any precedent within that month save for the last week exists to indicate that the event in question might occur, then the event itself will *not* be considered a surprise. The three weeks before the events in question are listed in Table 2.

Failure

The second aspect of the intervening variables is that of failure. Failure is necessary to the intervening variable so that a certain amount of negative feedback can be considered to be present. One possible way to determine whether negative feedback is present is to examine newspaper editorials for the period in question. These are chosen for reasons of comparability and their impact upon decision-makers. Our choice of newspapers includes a broad range of editorial opinion and policy that a president and his secretary of state is likely to read. Therefore, the following newspapers will be sampled: *Washington Post, Washington Evening Star, New York Herald Tribune, New York Times,* and *Wall Street Journal.* The list of newspapers is adapted from the work of Dan D. Nimmo.[49]

Failure will be measured by examining the various newspaper editorials about the crisis. They will be coded for negative affect only. We are not concerned with the advice they offer but only with the "judgment" that the decision-makers acted incorrectly in the situation under study. This coding will be done in a manner similar to that described for policy themes.

Only editorials on the crisis itself will be coded. After all these editorials have been coded, the editorial "scores" will be averaged. A crisis will be considered a failure only if 75 percent or more of the editorials judge that a president, secretary of state, or their representatives acted in error.

Newspapers tend to respond quickly to major events and to remain topical. Thus, the most appropriate sample dates will include the period of time from the onset of the crisis itself to the end of the crisis plus an additional two weeks. The two-week period is added to permit reflective editorials ("postmortems"), which usually follow major events.

The Dependent Variables

The dependent variables used in this study can be characterized as the "intellectual baggage" of a leader or decision-maker *after* a crisis that has been deemed a failure. Flexibility involves the difference in direction and intensity of goal and policy themes after a crisis has occurred. The difference in this case is measured as the change in these themes from the base period.

The hypotheses about degrees of flexibility and flexible behavior are tested by determining the distance between types of policy and goal themes for the two periods in ques-

TABLE 3

SAMPLE DATES FOR DEPENDENT VARIABLES

EVENT	SAMPLE DATES	
	First Date	Last Date
Czechoslovakia	Feb. 26,1948	Aug. 26,1948
PRC in Korea	Nov. 15,1950	May 15,1951
Hungary	Nov. 5,1956	May 5,1957
Lebanon	Aug. 4,1958	Feb. 4,1959
Berlin	Sep. 15,1961	Mar. 15,1962
Dominican Republic	May 1,1965	Nov. 1,1965
Tet Offensive	Feb. 2,1968	Aug. 3,1968
Mid East War	Oct. 24,1973	Apr. 24,1974

tion. This can be calculated in terms of aggregate scores and also by charting the behavior over time for each period and comparing the graphs. Since the intervening variables have been subject to strict inclusion and coding rules, we can be more confident that the findings indicating change are likely to be related to the sensitivity of a given leader.

Table 3 gives the sample dates for the dependent variables. This research procedure has certain implications that should be discussed. It has attempted to control for many variables that are usually considered to have an impact upon flexible behavior. By using several presidents and several secretaries of state, we have controlled for the role variable. By establishing objective measures of crisis and failure, we have controlled for differing types of crises. We have, moreover, added the requirement that the crisis be "other-inspired." By establishing these rules, a comparable series of cases has been established because all the cases have been subjected to the same inclusion rules.

It should therefore be possible to test the hypotheses. Even if these hypotheses are not supported, the research design still allows us to draw conclusions from our data. By including measures of incremental change, the possibility that events, especially crisis events, have no impact upon the behavior of leaders can be discovered and analyzed. By employing a comparative method, furthermore, we allow for the possibility of differential rates of change among leaders based on factors other than the ones identified.

4

What Crises Can We Study?

The first step is to determine which potential crises can be verified for each presidential administration since the end of World War II. This chapter presents the results of the crisis determination procedures and also the results of our investigation of failure in those crises.

Crisis Determination and Verification

Crisis has been defined as a situation of high threat, short time, and surprise, all three variables appearing simultaneously.[1] The operational definition of these variables has been adapted from the work of Thomas Brewer.[2] The first variable, that of high threat or high salience, is defined as a minimum of three *New York Times Index* entries per day about the crisis.[3] An additional requirement is that for any case to be considered high threat, a minimum of ten entries be found. Table 4 indicates the results of coding for high threat.[4]

The only possible crisis that did not seem to be perceived as a high threat was the PRC intervention in Korea in October 1950. Perhaps the crisis dates themselves were too inclusive, or perhaps the intervention was only one of several high salience events occurring during the period. Both explanations seem equally plausible. Logically, the intervention of the PRC in Korea was a single act, but what constitutes the possible crisis is not only the intervention per se but also the

TABLE 4

DETERMINING HIGH THREAT

EVENT	Total Entries	Entries/ Day
Czechoslovakia	18	3.0
PRC in Korea	64	2.13
Hungary	64	18.1
Lebanon	64	3.0
Berlin	367	11.1
Dominican Republic	25	4.16
Tet Offensive	68	6.8
Mid East War	412	18.72

reactions of the United States and the United Nations. Furthermore, the intervention occurred in the context of an ongoing crisis, the Korean War.[5] During October 1950 the Chinese intervention was one event in a chain of events affecting the Korean peninsula. For example, only seven days before the Chinese attacked, the United Nations was debating the wisdom of attacking across the thirty-eighth parallel.[6] Events in Korea were also moving at great speed, as the UN forces were sweeping north and destroying the remaining units of the North Korean army.[7] In short, this period did not lack fast-breaking news. It is possible, therefore, that the impact of the intervention was modified by other events taking place in Korea at that time.

Despite these explanations, however, the fact that the intervention does not meet the criteria of a high threat requires that we consider the case something other than a crisis. Thus, although the results for anticipation and short time will be reported for this case, the case itself will be excluded from further analysis.

The variable "short time" is defined in terms of real time (days, weeks) and the number of agencies involved in the decisions that are made (i.e., complexity). Time is considered short if the conditions under which a decision is to be made change negatively within a period of one month. Complexity requires a minimum of two agencies. Since all cases with which we are concerned involve at least two, they are considered sufficiently complex, and therefore, only the requirement that the conditions for a decision be less advantageous within one month need be determined.[8] All the cases were found to involve short time.

The final variable in determining crisis is that of anticipation. Events can be fully anticipated or come as a complete surprise. If an event is a surprise, it was completely unanticipated or there was no precedent for it. Anticipation is determined by examining a period of three weeks beginning one month before the event in question. The coding source for determining anticipation was the *New York Times Index.*[9] The definition of precedent requires some elaboration. An entry in the *Index* is considered a precedent if the entry refers to a statement made by the president, the secretary of state, or one of their representatives that they expect a certain action to occur. If a source outside the United States is responsible for a report during the period under examination and if that source does not meet any of the above criteria, that report is not considered a precedent.[10] Table 5 indicates the results determining surprise.

Of the cases first listed as having some face validity, only one has not been verified as a crisis. Not only did the Chinese intervention in Korea fail to meet the requirements for high threat, it was also anticipated. Several members of the administration as well as military commanders in the field discussed the possibility of Chinese intervention in the Korean conflict. In addition, several non-U.S. sources warned that the People's

TABLE 5

DETERMINING SURPRISE

EVENT	ANTICIPATION*
Czechoslovakia	S
PRC in Korea	A
Hungary	S
Lebanon	S
Berlin	S
Dominican Republic	S
Tet Offensive	S
Mid East War	S

* S = Surprise, A = Anticipated

Republic of China would take strong action if the military forces of the United States and the United Nations crossed the thirty-eighth parallel.[11] As Warren I. Cohen describes MacArthur's view of Chinese intervention, "Despite Chinese warnings that they would intervene if UN forces crossed the 38th Parallel, MacArthur remained confident that they would not dare—and that *if they did,* his forces would quickly destroy them. In mid-October, a nervous President flew to Wake Island to confer with his general and was assured that the war would be over by Thanksgiving."[12] It may be argued that the warnings received by Truman were not warnings at all, but were in reality assurances that the possibility of Chinese intervention would not in any way change the course of the Korean conflict. The fact remains, however, that the possibility of intervention was anticipated even though it was not taken seriously by some members of the administration. Thus, however one measures anticipation, it must be conceded that the intervention of the People's Liberation Army was not a surprise, even though the size of the forces and the success of the attackers did shock many officials in Truman's administration.

The verification of crisis by these empirical measures does not necessarily mean that all historical accounts of the events will agree that they constitute a crisis—perhaps because most historical accounts use the term *crisis* in a nonrigorous fashion. (It is not the purpose of this chapter to discuss the substance of the various crises and the individuals involved in these situations; I merely wish to indicate that when these situations are analyzed by operational definitions and rigorous coding rules, these events can at least be classified as crisis and non-crisis.)

Determining Failure in Crisis

Having verified a list of crises, we must now determine which of them were perceived as foreign policy failures, a task much more difficult than defining and operationalizing crisis. Failure, because of its psychological overtones, has defied definition and quantification by objective measures. Yet this inquiry demands that an objective indicator of subjective reality be found, that the particular objective indicators be selected from the vast spectrum of indicators available.

Initially, the most obvious and seemingly reliable approach in determining failure would be to survey those whom we wish to study and ask them to which media sources they paid attention. However, not all of these individuals are alive; moreover, selective recall would remain a problem for the rest even if they agreed to cooperate in the project. A second approach would be to determine an individual's probable reading materials by identifying the journals to which he subscribed. This approach has two problems. First, even if someone subscribes to a journal, it is by no means sure that he will read it. Second, information about subscription lists is often unavailable.[13] We do, however, have some empirical evidence that permits a sampling procedure to determine failure. In his study of public information officers in the federal government, Dan D. Nimmo found that these individuals receive much of their information about public opinion from newspaper editorials.[14] Nimmo's findings are supported by Karl Deutsch, who names the mass media as one of the sources of elite opinion.[15] Still other scholars have examined the role of the media in foreign policy and have found that they serve an opinion-making function.[16] Nimmo, furthermore, quotes a public information officer as typical not only of the role of editorial opinion but also of the selectivity of opinion on the part of a large percentage of government officials.

> Every morning at five o'clock I have men come in the office and go through the following newspapers: *The Washington Post, The* [Washington] *Daily News,* the *New York Herald Tribune,* the *New York Times,* and the *Wall Street Journal.* We have found that stories being run in these newspapers are generally those important in many other areas of the country. Furthermore, from the standpoint of editorial opinion, these six or seven newspapers cover the entire spectrum politically, from conservative on through liberal. . . . They represent an opinion of particular importance to policy officials, that is those that will be read by many officials other than those in this department and by many segments of the public which will be interested in policy.[17]

Nimmo's list of publications has been used to determine failure, with the exception of the *Washington Daily News.*[18]

Failure is determined by coding the editorials in these newspapers during the period of the crisis plus two weeks after its resolution. The addition of two weeks at the end of the crisis period enables the coder to examine the summary editorial that usually follows the culmination of a crisis.[19] If 75 percent of the newspapers examined are critical of the presidential administration's handling of the crisis, this handling will be considered a failure.

The calculation of the failure scores needs further elaboration. These scores are calculated by determining which newspapers were published at the time and were passing an opinion on the crisis. In the last few crises, for example, the *New York Herald Tribune* was no longer being published; therefore our sample for these crises was four newspapers rather than five.

Newspaper editors, however, although they tend to comment on most important issues, do not always take a definitive stand. In certain cases, an editorial may merely comment that a particular situation is dangerous or important without assigning fault or praise. In these cases, the editorial is considered of neutral affect. The following *New York Herald Tribune* editorial on Hungary illustrates a neutral affect.

> Somber as the news from Hungary is, the free world can only take hope from the courageous resistance of the Hungarian people. So overwhelming is the military superiority of the advancing Soviet Russian armies, and so ruthless is Moscow's disregard of all human and moral considerations, that a Soviet triumph may well be inevitable. . . .
>
> But the valiant men and women of Hungary have given an answer. . . . It is the answer of a people who will fight and die, if need be, for national integrity and individual liberty. It is an answer which may be crushed today but which will rise again tomorrow.[20]

In the opinion of the *Herald Tribune,* no one in the administration is to be praised or condemned, only the Hungarians are praised. The *Washington Post*'s editorial during the Berlin crisis is another example of neutral affect.

> The Berlin crisis is developing with fidelity to the script which previous history has written for the classic diplomatic buildup of Twentieth Century international crises. Secretary Rusk's acknowledgement that there will be negotiations probably later this month is in the tradition.
>
> This has been the dreary plot of this generation's foreign

affairs spectaculars. . . .

The prospect of negotiations ought to diminish no one's apprehensions. The testing time over Berlin still is to come. The moment for real decisions has not been reached. Yet it helps to know that the best, thus far, at least, has not forgotten the lines by which power diplomacy has been played out in crisis after crisis without so far plunging the world into war.[21]

Similarly, when there are as many editorials of positive affect as of negative affect, the newspaper is deemed "neutral." When a newspaper in the sample is considered neutral, failure is calculated by a percentage of all newspapers that are not deemed neutral. In the Lebanese crisis of 1958, the *Washington Evening Star* and the *New York Times* were both, on balance, neutral.[22] The three remaining newspapers were critical of the Eisenhower administration. Consequently, its handling of the crisis can be considered a failure.[23] The failure score for the Lebanese crisis is therefore 100 percent, since three of the three newspapers taking a definite stand were critical.

For proper coding of editorials, it was necessary to identify all editorials about the crisis during the sample period. After identifying each editorial, the targets of the editorial were determined. Only when the targets of the editorial were the president, the secretary of state, the "administration," or the American public were the editorials used to calculate failure. In editorials in which a wide variety of targets was mentioned, only those statements that pertained to the president, the secretary of state, and so forth were coded. Thus, if an editorial on Berlin condemned Khrushchev and praised the people of West Berlin but only mentioned the actions of the Kennedy administration, that editorial would be coded as neutral toward the Kennedy administration.[24] One result of this criterion was to reduce the number of editorials that could be coded. During the Lebanese crisis, for example, the

took a stand were critical. This distribution is the same for
the Tet offensive but not for the Dominican Republic. The
choice of Tet, therefore, allows us a more homogeneous intervening variable, one in which variations between independent and dependent variables are unlikely to be caused by
variation within the intervening variable. Third, Tet seems
more of a crisis and more dramatic a failure than the Dominican intervention. In the Dominican Republic, the United
States policy seems to have evolved by small decisions and
small mistakes. As A. F. Lowenthal puts it, "the Dominican
intervention was not the simple outcome of the U.S. government's single-minded pursuit of national objective. . . . The
. . . intervention resulted . . . from a complex of decisions and
actions on lesser matters by various American officials up and
down the line none of whom seemed to have expected or
wished his decisions to lead to military intervention."[25] In addition to becoming involved in the Dominican Republic by
accident (perhaps because foreign policy leaders were paying
more attention to Vietnam by 1965), the United States
seems to have become involved there because many foreign
policy decision-makers believed that the Dominican people
and their revolutionary leaders had had no experience with
democracy and must therefore be instructed by wise U.S.
policy. In the words of W. Howard Wriggins, "As for U.S.
policy, it may be possible by prompt and generous economic
assistance to tide a new regime over its most difficult period.
. . . If the new men have had little experience governing,
there may be advisors who can help to bring the voice of
wider experience to their assistance."[26] Not only is the image
of poor ill-advised leaders in backward countries somewhat
different from that of North Vietnamese aggression, but the
Dominican crisis also occurred in an area where the United
States traditionally considers itself the leading power. In contrast, the Tet offensive occurred under much different circumstances. The total impact of the Tet offensive is perhaps
best described by Robert Shaplen:

By their unique and audacious attacks of late January and the first weeks of February on Saigon and Hue and some thirty other provincial capitals, along with seventy district towns throughout South Vietnam, the Communists have suddenly altered the nature and the course of the whole long and painful war here and, at least momentarily, are in a stronger position than ever before to set their own terms for negotiation.[27]

Thus, on the basis of both quantitative and qualitative analysis, the choice of the Tet offensive over the Dominican crisis seems justified.

We have also eliminated the Hungarian Crisis of 1956. This situation, although it was a crisis, cannot be considered a failure, primarily because a sense developed at that time that the United States was powerless to help the Hungarian rebels without starting a nuclear war with the Soviet Union. Eisenhower's own statements about the events of October and November 1956 sum up the dilemma that he and the United States faced:

The twin problems of Hungary and Suez now became more acute and, in addition, created an anomalous situation. In Europe we were aligned with Britain and France in our opposition to the brutal Soviet invasion of Hungary; in the Middle East we were against the entry of British-French armed forces in Egypt. . . .

The Hungarian uprising, from its beginning to its bloody suppression, was an occurrence that inspired in our nation feelings of sympathy and admiration for the rebels, anger and disgust for their Soviet oppressors. . . . An expedition combining West German or Italian forces with our own, and moving across neutral Austria, Titoist Yugoslavia, or Communist Czechoslovakia, was out of the question. . . . Unless the major nations of Europe would, without delay, ally themselves spontaneously with us (an unimaginable prospect), we could do nothing. Sending United States troops alone into Hungary through hostile or neutral territory would have involved us in a general war.[28]

This view of the Hungarian problem—compounded as it was by both geography and the Suez crisis—seems to have been generally accepted at the time. Thus, the Hungarian crisis was a problem without an active solution; Eisenhower did not act, which in general was the best decision he could make.

As a result of the coding procedures for failure, an interesting pattern developed. Each administration had at least one crisis that was criticized by all the sampled newspapers that stated a definite opinion. When viewed in relation to the independent and dependent variables, i.e., to the mental sets of decision-makers, this finding is most encouraging. For example, if one newspaper agreed with the president's actions in a certain crisis and all other newspapers were critical, one could argue that this president was concerned only with the opinion of the one newspaper in question. Since it agreed with his policy decision, there was no reason for the president to change his referents, goal theme, or policy theme after the crisis. These findings make that argument a moot one.

A final question arises in the context of failure coding, that of the spread of opinion within each newspaper in the sample. Table 7 presents the number of editorials of each type for each newspaper for each crisis.

As Table 7 indicates, crises that have been deemed failures are failures both in terms of each newspaper and in terms of total percentages of editorials on a given crisis. The Berlin crisis has more individual positive editorials than any other crisis that has been deemed a failure. Yet even for Berlin, there are still more negative than positive editorials.

The procedures used to determine crisis and failure resulted in the elimination of two of the possible cases: the Chinese intervention in Korea and the Hungarian uprising. The former was eliminated because it could not be verified as a crisis, the latter because it could not be considered a failure. Finally, the intervention of the United States in the Dominican Republic was also eliminated because there was

TABLE 7

INDIVIDUAL NEWSPAPER SCORES

EVENT	WP			WES			NYHT			NYT			WSJ		
	-	N	+	-	N	+	-	N	+	-	N	+	-	N	+
Czechoslovakia	2	1	0	3	1	0	0	1	0	1	0	0	-	-	-
Hungary	0	2	1	0	0	2	3	2	1	0	2	3	-	-	-
Lebanon	5	1	0	0	3	0	2	0	1	1	4	1	1	0	0
Berlin	0	4	0	3	1	3	2	2	1	1	2	1	5	0	0
Dominican Republic	3	0	0	2	1	1	2	0	0	5	0	0	0	0	2
Tet Offensive	3	0	0	1	1	0	-	-	-	3	1	0	0	3	0
Mid East War	1	3	1	3	3	2	-	-	-	7	3	1	2	0	1

WP	= Washington Post	-	= Negative Affect
WES	= Washington Evening Star	N	= Neutral
NYHT	= New York Herald Tribune	+	= Positive Affect
NYT	= New York Times		
WSJ	= Wall Street Journal		

a second case, which seemed relatively more of a crisis and at the same time more of a failure. The cases that will be examined for each president are the subject of the next chapter.

5

A View of Individuals in
Foreign Policy Crises

The present study compares and assesses the flexibility exhibited by selected decision-makers before and after a crisis that has been deemed a failure. It differs from other studies of foreign policy not so much in the questions that are asked about how the decision-makers react, but in the procedures used to answer them. This chapter provides brief but necessary information about the selected cases and the circumstances surrounding the decisions that were reached.[1]

Czechoslovakia: The Haberdasher and His General

The first crisis is the March 1948 coup in Czechoslovakia and the Truman administration's reaction to it. The interaction of the events themselves and Truman and Marshall have been the subject of considerable study and analysis. Several questions can be raised about the nature of the case, which gives an indication of the differences in approach and assumptions used by several scholars. Was the coup so symbolic—marking as it did the complete subjugation of Eastern Europe and a watershed in the Cold War—that the United States should have reacted to it with all the military power at its command? Was the coup itself unimportant, becoming significant only because Truman saw it as a way to advance his other foreign policy initiatives? Was the coup itself a reaction to earlier threatening actions taken by the United States

toward the Soviet Union? Was the coup inspired by the
Soviet Union? If so, did it merely complete a Soviet sphere of
influence and "buffer zone," or was it part of a larger plan to
subjugate all of Europe?

No definite answer can be given to any of these questions. They all involve a series of assumptions about foreign
policy relationships in 1948 as well as in the years before.
They tend to use the same "facts" to reach very different
conclusions. But beyond the fact that before March 1948
Czechoslovakia had a noncommunist government and after
March 1948 a communist-controlled government, scholarly
analysis tends to consist of logical deductions from, or impres-
sions of, the situation.

The coup in Czechoslovakia began when the Czechoslovak minister of the interior began to purge noncommunist
police officers. According to many scholars, this purge was
undertaken in preparation for the elections scheduled for
May 1948.[2] The purge of the police led to the resignation of
the noncommunist cabinet ministers, which in turn marked
the beginning of the communist takeover of the entire country. From this series of events Herbert Feis concluded that
the coup in Czechoslovakia was the last straw for the United
States and that from then on the West would take a much
stronger position vis-à-vis the Soviet Union:

> The tragic death of Masaryk, coming after Benes sad submis-
> sion, gave an emotional tone to the Western reaction to this
> Communist coup. Sympathy for these two victims of Commu-
> nist persecution, esteemed for their good will and lofty
> natures, was fused with indignation at the methods used, and
> anger over the upset of the last remaining democratic and
> friendly government in Central Europe.
>
> The coursing emotion gave impetus to strong and bold
> measures of the Western governments cohesively to deter or
> offset any further Communist attempts by whatever means—
> conventional, subversive, or forcible—to extend their power
> into Western Europe or the Mediterranean.[3]

The notion that Czechoslovakia had been "raped" by the communists led some commentators to believe that the United States must react firmly to this situation. A typical reaction is an editorial from the *Washington Post*:

> The most important news in the world today, in our opinion, is the report that the United States, Great Britain, and France are exploring means of halting the spread of Soviet tyranny. There is no room for doubt that these large democratic powers and their neighbors can turn the tide of Soviet aggression if they properly unite for that purpose. . . . The joint protest against the rape of Czechoslovakia was a beginning. Yet every realist knows that the time for words has passed. Bold strokes seem to be the only present hope of arresting the police-state menace without a major war.[4]

The *Washington Post*'s recommendation was a quick enactment of the Marshall Plan.[5] Feis echoed this thought when he claimed that as a result of the Czechoslovak coup, many measures, "conjoined with the Marshall Plan program, creat[ing] a connected Western common front."[6] In short, many believed that the Czechoslovakian situation was a catalyst for several related developments in postwar Europe.

This view, however, regardless of its emotional appeal, is not the only interpretation of the events in Czechoslovakia. Rather than viewing this episode as the *first* event in a chain of events, other scholars see Czechoslovakia as the *culmination* of a series of episodes that began after the announcement of the Truman Doctrine. The events in Hungary and Czechoslovakia are seen as an attempt by the Soviet Union to protect itself against the policies of the United States. For example, David Horowitz sees the expansionist policy of the Soviet Union as a reaction to Western initiatives such as the Truman Doctrine and the Marshall Plan:[7] "The whole postwar United States policy of facing the Soviets with an 'iron fist' and 'strong language,' while at the same time making it difficult as possible for them to carry out the work of reconstruction, virtually ensured the 'expansion' that the policy, allegedly, had been designed to prevent."[8] Viewed in this way, the coup in Czechoslovakia was the result of the earlier behavior of the United States and should have come as no surprise to anyone. If we adopt this view of events, the Truman administration is cast in the role of the "villain," utilizing its superior capabilities to precipitate a United States-Soviet schism after the end of World War II. The notion that the United States is responsible for the Cold War is given further support by the finding that the United States initiated many more conflict acts during the late 1940s and early 1950s than did the Soviet Union.[9] The actions of the Soviet Union in Czechoslovakia, therefore, were allegedly defensive in nature, and the policies of the United States were expansionist.

A third interpretation of these events is also possible. This interpretation assigns blame neither to the Soviet Union nor to the United States but does contend that the events gave Truman a great opportunity to push programs to which he was committed. Thus, it is argued, the Czech coup gave impetus to the signing of the Brussels pact.[10] Regardless of the motives of either major power, the coup was a heaven-sent opportunity for Truman to press for both the European Recovery Program and the defense arrangements that ultimately led to the creation of NATO in 1949.

The actions and reactions of the individuals involved in these events are also subject to widely divergent interpretations. It seems even more difficult to agree on the motives of President Truman and Secretary of State George C. Marshall than it is to agree on the "real" importance of the Czechoslovak coup. In order to examine the question of motives, one must first determine what the individual's dominant view was, because an individual is likely to "fit" a new situation into a preestablished pattern of behavior whenever possible.[11]

In the case of President Truman, it can be argued that he

was violently anticommunist throughout his presidency and that he was likely to react sternly to the events in Czechoslovakia. After all, had he not been a strong supporter of aid to Greece and Turkey? Had these policies and his attitude toward the events in Iran not begun a series of moves—from the Truman Doctrine through the Marshall Plan to the organization of NATO? His dislike and mistrust of the Soviet Union can be traced back beyond the 1948 Czech coup. His response to the situation in Greece and Turkey can be considered typical. He demanded several times that the State Department rework the speech he would give the Congress in order to point out clearly the policy he wished them to follow.

> I returned this draft to Acheson with a note asking for more emphasis on a declaration of general policy. The department's draftsmen then rewrote the speech to include a general policy statement, but it still seemed to me half-hearted. . . . I took my pencil, scratched out "should" and wrote in "must." In several other places I did the same thing; I wanted no hedging in this speech. This was America's answer to the surge of expansion of Communist tyranny. It had to be clear and free of hesitation or double talk.[12]

This statement suggests that during this period Truman was likely to resist Soviet expansion in any way possible. He may have felt unable to act in Czechoslovakia because of its proximity to the Soviet Union, but it does seem clear that the coup did give the opportunity he needed to develop public support for his policies of containment and the strengthening of Europe. On April 1, 1948, Truman declared that if the world desired peace and security, it was necessary to support the European Recovery Plan, strengthen the Pan-American Union, and resist communist expansion.[13]

Truman, then, can be viewed as one who acted according to the principle that communist expansion was evil and dangerous and had to be fought by all means possible, including economic and military means. In fact, Truman seems to have thought that economic solutions to communist expansion were just as important as security arrangements.[14] We can conclude that regardless of the motivation behind his behavior, Truman saw Czechoslovakia as the type of situation that merited a spirited response—not because it was an opportunity to speed up passage of the ERP or because it was truly a critical event. Rather, the coup enabled Truman to continue a series of policies that led to what has been termed the "Cold War."

Truman had great faith in his secretary of state, George C. Marshall. Marshall's war record and his global reputation served him very well as the chief foreign affairs officer in the United States at the time. He added luster to the foreign policies of a new president who was himself not widely known. Years after the coup in Czechoslovakia, President Truman claimed that Marshall would "go down in history as one of the great men of his time."[15] Marshall had Truman's complete confidence, and his opinion and assessment of the Czechoslovak situation are helpful in determining the "real" motives and policies of the Truman administration.

Marshall was not universally admired by all decision-makers in Washington during his public career. Perhaps Senator Joseph McCarthy expressed the most extreme criticism: "It was the Truman branch of the Democratic Party meeting at Denver, Colorado, which named the men responsible for the disaster which they called a 'great victory'— Dean Gooderham Acheson and George Catlett Marshall. By what tortured reasoning they arrived at the conclusion that the loss of 100 million people a year to Communism was a 'great victory' was unexplained."[16] But if we discount McCarthy, as we probably can, we find that the secretary was generally respected both for his grasp of complex problems and his ability to deal with these problems in a creative way. This seems to be the case with the Czechoslovakian coup and its aftermath. As George Kennan described the situation in Czechoslovakia at the time:

The halt in the Communist advance, I considered, had placed the Communists before the necessity of consolidating their power through Eastern Europe. For this reason they would soon find themselves obliged to clamp down entirely on Czechoslovakia. So long as Communist power had been advancing generally in Europe, it had been to Russian advantage to allow to the Czechs the outward appearances of freedom; but now that the advance had been halted, they could no longer afford the luxury. . . . I invite attention particularly to the passage about Czechoslovakia. The analysis proved correct. The crisis in that country came three and a half months later and culminated, as is well known, with the discarding of the last trappings of true democracy and the establishment of an unadulterated Communist dictatorship. Actually, as is readily apparent from the above, this development represented a defensive reaction—and one foreseen by ourselves—to the success of the Marshall Plan initiative. This, however, was understood neither by American opinion nor by the people throughout our governmental bureaucracy. The result was that the Communist crackdown in Czechoslovakia, when it came, was received generally as a new Communist success—the evidence, in fact, of the inadequacy of the methods of containment employed up to that time. This had, as we shall see . . . an effect on the origins of the NATO pact and on that militarization of thinking about the cold war generally that would overtake official Washington in the coming period.[17]

As head of the policy planning council in the State Department, Kennan had direct access to Marshall during this period, and at least three and a half months before March 1948, Marshall was aware of the reports about the possible "fall" of Czechoslovakia and the probable reasons for it. The fact that the coup itself led to a hardening of United States attitudes toward the Soviet Union can be viewed as a benefit or a liability, but from Kennan's standpoint, the United States could not and should not view the coup in Czechoslovakia as a provocation on the part of the USSR.

The question remains, however: which interpretation of

the events and personalities involved in the Czech coup seems best to fit the facts? The answer depends upon one's prejudices and the inferences one is willing to draw from the facts. Thus we know very little about the crisis itself in terms of its effects on the decision-makers in our study.

Lebanon: The Golfer and His Deacon

Critics of the United States point to the 1958 crisis with great derision. The United States, a world power with a great variety of resources at its disposal, reverted to a tactic that usually does very little to improve its image abroad. In short, Eisenhower employed "gunboat diplomacy" and "sent in the Marines." Why was it necessary to send any troops at all into this area in 1958 when similar circumstances did not lead to the dispatch of troops in 1976? Why did the troops stay so long in Lebanon? Why did Dulles and Eisenhower support the government of Lebanon rather than reverse the effects of the coup in Iraq? Erich Hula gives the following description of events in the Middle East at that time:

> The Middle Eastern crisis of 1958 . . . focused on Lebanon and Jordan. It was of a less serious nature than the Suez crisis but the lesson it taught was hardly less significant. In the first place, it was an American action this time, the landing of our Marines on the shores of Lebanon, that aroused strong opposition in the United Nations. . . . We were sincerely convinced that we had to comply with the request of the lawful Lebanese government, friendly to us though not formally allied with us, to assist it against domestic subversive forces aided from abroad, not only because we had ourselves a stake in the maintaining of the Middle Eastern *status quo* but also because we felt our action was required in order to assure respect for the purposes and principles of the Charter. But it was nonetheless not unlikely that our own appraisal of the situation and our choice of the means of meeting it would be challenged, and not merely by members of the Soviet bloc. In fact, the political necessity and wisdom of the action were also seriously

questioned by large sections of American public opinion itself.[18]

In addition, it must be remembered that this was also the time of the coup in Iraq and the advancement of Nasser-style politics in the region as a whole.

The situation in Lebanon was unclear from the outset, and Eisenhower and Dulles did little if anything to clear up the confusion, which led to a negative reaction among many segments of public opinion in the United States. Eisenhower himself recounted the decision process that took place during this time:

Behind everything was our deep-seated conviction that the Communists were principally responsible for the trouble, and that the President Chamoun was motivated only by a strong feeling of patriotism. . . .

On the morning of May 13 I met with Secretary Foster Dulles and others to discuss a communication from President Chamoun inquiring as to "what our actions would be if he were to request our assistance." We met in a climate of impatience because of our belief that Chamoun's uneasiness was the result of one more Communist provocation. Although temporarily pursuing a "soft" propaganada line, the Soviets were pushing everywhere, stirring up trouble in Venezuela, Indonesia, and Burma, not to mention the Middle East. . . . Foster Dulles felt that if we should send troops into Lebanon there would be a major adverse reaction in the Middle East. . . . Possible Soviet reaction was another item to consider. This point did not worry me excessively; I believed the Soviets would not take action if the United States movements were decisive and strong particularly if other parts of the Middle East were not involved in the operations. . . .

Obviously the decision to send troops to Lebanon was not one to be taken lightly. In review, as is normal in decisions involving operations of war, the problem was to select the least objectionable of several possible courses of action.[19]

This decision was based on a "deep-seated conviction." Whether hard evidence was available to support that conviction is not at all clear from Eisenhower's assessment of the situation. If we assume that a statesman writing his memoirs will try to describe events in their most positive light, this omission in Eisenhower's memoirs is all the more puzzling. Secretary of State Dulles accepted the notion of communist infiltration but listed an additional reason for the dispatch of U.S. armed forces to the area:

> Our decision to move troops into Lebanon, which was made within a few hours without enough time for adequate explanation, was made for one reason, and one reason alone. We were convinced that if we did not, there would not be a single one of the small and relatively weak governments all the way from Morocco to the Pacific which would feel safe from the potential threat of individual aggression and assassination such as took place in Iraq. We acted to give a feeling of stability to such governments so that they would not automatically collapse, or feel that to be a friend of the United States was a liability in terms of independence or of life itself.[20]

Given the statements of Eisenhower and the perceptions of Dulles, we can conclude that the Lebanese intervention was apparently undertaken to emphasize the U.S. commitment to protect small states from communist aggression. Other research has indicated, however, that Dulles, as the chief architect of American policy at this time, did nothing to test reality but merely interpreted events as reinforcing his view that the Soviet Union was a malevolent force in world affairs.[21] Thus, it is difficult if not impossible to determine in any empirical way whether Eisenhower and Dulles were justified in sending troops to Lebanon. The relationship between Dulles and Eisenhower also deserves to be discussed. For most of the Eisenhower administration, Dulles was the chief foreign policy decision-maker. Eisenhower's well-known desire to delegate authority also went far in making Dulles's attitudes and policy choices central to foreign policy determination.

In addition to the decision to send troops to Lebanon—ostensibly to protect American citizens—the question of the number of troops sent and the amount of time they spent there make the nature and purpose of the intervention even more ambiguous. An editorial in the *Wall Street Journal* illustrates the problem:

> Whatever else the armed intervention in Lebanon may show the world about the United States, it is a clear demonstration that we have failed to find any other policy for the Middle East. Were this not so, we would not now be using troops. . . . President Eisenhower decided that all else having failed there was no other course except armed intervention to prevent the loss of other governments to the Pan-Arabism symbolized by Mr. Nasser.
>
> That this was an act of desperation to save what remains of our position in the Middle East is clear from the risks we accepted.[22]

Thus, according to the *Wall Street Journal,* the only logical explanation of the troop movements was as an effort to salvage a policy that had not been thought out. The editorial does not even mention the protection of United States citizens as a pretext for the intervention.

Overall, the U.S. intervention in Lebanon seems to have been based on assumptions about the Middle East that can be questioned without too much difficulty. Furthermore, it is nearly impossible to have any confidence in the assignment of motives either to Eisenhower or Dulles. Each seems to have given a slightly different version of the facts that led to the decision to intervene and of the reasons for the intervention itself. In the case of Dulles, his perception of reality, especially in cases where the Soviet Union was either directly or indirectly involved, was biased. Thus, the Lebanese case is even more confused and confusing than is the Czechoslovak coup.

Berlin: Camelot's King and Clerk

The events in and around Berlin in 1961 are the Kennedy administration's crisis failure. The Berlin crisis, including the construction of the "Wall," was as major a shock to the newly installed administration as other events at the same time, such as the "Bay of Pigs" fiasco. Berlin, however, must be evaluated not only in terms of its impact on the Kennedy administration but also in terms of the motives and aims of the Soviet Union. Raymond Garthoff, for example, believes that Berlin showed the weakness of the USSR.

> By 1961, when their [the Soviets'] second major push on Berlin was proving unsuccessful, they did, to be sure, build "the wall." But this was a fallback position on their part to deal with some of the more desperate problems of East Germany, and not part of a preferred strategy of evicting us from West Berlin. They have continued intermittently to keep the Berlin issue alive. Nonetheless, it has been six years since the Soviets, in November 1958, gave us six months to agree to a changed status of West Berlin, and in this time they have been unable to force us to do so.[23]

The legal rights of the United States, the United Kingdom, and France in Berlin and their access to Berlin were not in question. Basic agreement on these matters had been reached in the past. The Berlin crisis was not over access itself but rather over the announced intention of the Soviet Union to sign a separate peace treaty with the German Democratic Republic (East Germany) and thereby to give the East Germans, rather than the Soviets, control of traffic to and from West Berlin. This change was unacceptable to the United States. The problem of East German refugees' pouring into West Berlin was another problem, but it tended to be secondary. These problems were made more complex by the realization that acceptance of the Soviet position would lead to the de facto recognition of East Germany and the formalization of the East-West division of that country. As a result,

Washington began to feel that the Soviet Union had begun a major crisis, one that involved the peace and future of the world. It gave little or no thought to the possibility that the Soviet position on Berlin was predicated on internal problems in East Germany.

Arthur M. Schlesinger, Jr. describes Kennedy's attitude toward the crisis:

> The President [Kennedy] was meanwhile fighting his way through the thicket of debate to his own conclusions. Cuba and Laos had been side issues. But Berlin threatened a war which might destroy civilization, and he thought about little else that summer. Stewart Udall, trying to talk to him about conservation remarked, "He's imprisoned by Berlin." One afternoon after a meeting with the Joint Chiefs of Staff, the President talked at some length with James Wechsler of the *New York Post.* Only "fools," Kennedy said, could cling to the idea of victory in a nuclear war. A once-and-for-all peace seemed quite unlikely. . . . This meant that the United States would not give way and, if the Soviet Union persisted in its determination to destroy the freedom of West Berlin, we would be prepared to go to war, even nuclear war. But while Kennedy wanted to make this resolve absolutely clear to Moscow, he wanted to make it equally clear that we were not, as he once put it to me, "war-mad."[24]

For Kennedy, therefore, Berlin was of crucial importance: the issue was nothing less than the survival of the human race. Benjamin Bradlee also testifies to Kennedy's stark view of the situation. As he describes the grim meeting that took place in Vienna preceding the Berlin crisis:

> All jocularity disappeared at the third Kennedy-Khrushchev session, requested by the president to nail down the Soviet position on Berlin. "This was the nut-cutter," Kennedy said more than once later. The president told Khrushchev it was not so much the Soviet determination to sign a separate peace treaty with East Germany that bothered him, as it was the Soviet

interpretation that such a treaty would make West Berlin irrevocably East German. That was not acceptable to the United
States. Acceptable or not, Khrushchev thundered back, it was
going to happen—in December, six months later. "If the U.S.
wanted to go to war," Kennedy quoted Khrushchev slowly,
"that's your business, but you must understand that force will
be met with force." Kennedy said he replied "It looks like a
cold winter."[25]

Was Kennedy justified in his assessment of the situation?
After all, a war did not start over the Berlin question, and
most scholars would agree that the Soviet Union backed
down. Did it retreat because of the stakes that Kennedy assigned to the issues, or did it change its tactics because the
question of Berlin was not crucial to their overall policy at
the time? As Geoffrey Stern argues, was the real issue in the
Berlin episode the recognition of Soviet hegemony over all of
Eastern Europe?[26]

The problem here is not one of factual discrepancies but
interpretation of fact. We know that a crisis occurred. We
know that it ended, but we cannot be sure what caused the
crisis or why it ended so abruptly. We know from all measures of activity during this period that a crisis existed,[27] but
we do not know why all the events in question tended to
appear with great rapidity in the summer of 1961.

As we have seen, Kennedy's thoughts and policies on
Berlin shed little if any light on the various motives involved
in the crisis. Perhaps the activities and attitudes of Secretary
of State Rusk may be useful in this respect. As far as it is
possible to determine, Rusk's attitude toward and suggestions
about Berlin are more obscure than enlightening. First, as has
often been poined out,[28] Rusk under Kennedy was much
more an administrative officer than a policy planner (as we
shall see the reverse was true during the Johnson-Rusk era).
Kennedy, it seems, wished to take a personal hand in the
foreign policy process, and Rusk's function was to implement
his decisions. Thus, even if Rusk's views on Berlin could be

easily determined, their value as evidence must be carefully assessed. In fact, Rusk's views on Berlin are difficult to determine. Schlesinger goes so far as to say that "Rusk was circumspect, and no one quite knew where he stood."[29] Rusk's most definite position was his statement at a session of the National Security Council: on July 13, 1961, "Rusk reaffirmed the Acheson argument that we should not negotiate until the crisis became more acute."[30] Surely this is a less than dramatic statement. In view of the role Rusk held in the Kennedy administration, the lack of information about his views on the Berlin situation does not seem at all surprising.

There is too little evidence to make a satisfying evaluation of American behavior in the Berlin crisis. In addition, it is virtually impossible to make any generalizations based on this one case. This conclusion is supported by quantitative analysis of this situation.[31] In short, the Berlin crisis, like the crises that have already been discussed, does not yield the type of information we need for our research design if we confine our search for information to the standard academic and popular literature.

Tet: The Domestic Politician and His Foreign Advisor

The Johnson administration not only became entangled in the most divisive war in the history of the United States, it also displayed a marked incompetence in coping with the details of combat. It is in this larger context of the war that the failure surrounding the Tet offensive must be viewed. The war served not only as a catalyst for much of the domestic discontent that subsequently developed in the United States but also indicated that over 500,000 men and vast amounts of modern equipment were not enough to protect the population centers of South Vietnam or develop political support for the Saigon regime. In short, the American involvement in the conflict was a tragic loss of men and material. Why was the Johnson administration so ill prepared to meet the Tet offensive? Why were so many well-equipped men unable to establish anything like safe zones against guerrilla forces? Why was the American psychological reaction to the situation in Vietnam so massive? Why did American public opinion force the Johnson administration from office not long after the Tet offensive?

The facts of the Tet offensive are not in dispute. The North Vietnamese and the Viet Cong staged a massive attack on provincial capitals as well as military bases in Vietnam in January and early February 1968.

> By their unique and audacious attacks of late January and the first weeks of February on Saigon and Hue and some thirty other provincial capitals, along with seventy districts and towns throughout South Vietnam, the Communists have suddenly altered the nature and course of the whole long and painful conflict here and, at least momentarily, are in a stronger position than ever before to set their own terms for negotiation. Nevertheless, it remains questionable whether the North Vietnamese and Viet Cong strategists will succeed in their daring gamble . . . whatever degree of success or failure they may be judged to have—cost the Viet Cong heavily.[32]

The attacks themselves cannot be evaluated in purely military terms, because they were not intended for purely military purposes. In fact, it could be argued that for North Vietnam, the military objectives per se were minor and the psychological, the diplomatic objectives of major importance. If so, then the success or failure of either side cannot be judged by the amount of territory seized or the number of casualties inflicted. Rather the offensive can be considered as a major North Vietnamese triumph—if its purpose was primarily political and if the political demise of Lyndon Johnson was attributable in large measure to the effects that the offensive had on the American public. Viewed in this light, Tet becomes a major failure to the Johnson administration and more importantly to Johnson himself.

In this case, Johnson's leadership style becomes rather

important. According to James David Barber, Johnson can be termed an active-negative president, a type Barber defines as follows:

> *Active-negative.* The basic contradiction is between relatively intense effort and relatively low personal reward for that effort. The activity has a compulsive quality; politics appears as a means for compensating for power deprivations through ambitious striving. The stance toward the environment is aggressive and the problem of managing aggressive feelings is persistent. The self-image is typically vague and temporally discontinuous. Life is a hard struggle to achieve and hold power, hampered by the condemnations of a perfectionistic conscience.[33]

Barber not only gives a general definition of an active-negative president but also singles out Johnson for special analysis: "It would be tedious to document President Lyndon B. Johnson's difficulties in personal relations. The bully-raging, the humiliations visited upon the men around him, are nearly as familiar as his rages against the Kennedy clan. By mid-1966 it was hard to find an independent voice among his intimate advisors."[34] Could a man who had this attitude toward his role and his advisers view the Tet situation as anything but a failure? Could he not also have directed his rage at his advisors and at the North Vietnamese? And would not his inability to justify these occurrences to himself ultimately lead to his decision to withdraw from political life?

All these questions could be answered in the affirmative, but if we did so, we would have to recognize the possibility that Johnson himself thought the Tet offensive was a failure. No such evidence exists save for the fact that he did withdraw from the presidential race. But can his withdrawal be viewed as conclusive evidence that he recognized Tet as a failure? It may be said that Johnson did not seek another term because he felt that he would be unable to win the election, but withdrawal is by no means equivalent to an admission of failure vis-à-vis Tet. It may be argued that John-son assumed he would lose the election because the public was upset about the conduct of war in general. That, how-ever, is not specific to the events in January and February of 1968. Finally, even if his decision not to run was based on all the factors mentioned above, that does not mean that he thought that he was wrong. Rather, he could have been making a very calculated judgment based on the popular opinion polls.

One fact is certain: Johnson chose not to run. This choice is in contradiction to earlier choices he is believed to have made. In this sense, his behavior seems to be rather flexible—even given our definition of flexibility. The crucial word in the previous statements is *seems.* That one decision—which may be more domestic than foreign in nature—is but one act (regardless how important it may be) among a series of ac-tions Johnson took during this period. There is no empirical support for the notion that Johnson's decision not to run for reelection was typical of his actions at that time. Thus, al-though one can discuss the issue involved in the Tet offensive more distinctly than in the preceding cases, we must research the degree of flexibility in and after that crisis more rigorous-ly before any firm conclusions can be reached.

In the case of Secretary of State Rusk, different ques-tions must be asked. It has to be remembered that this is the second time Rusk appears: but Vietnam was obviously quite different from Berlin, and the superior to whom he reported had changed. These factors must be taken into account be-fore we can discuss Rusk's behavior before and after each crisis. Perhaps most important, however, are the relationships between Kennedy and Rusk and between Johnson and Rusk. If we wish to obtain any reasonable picture of the interplay of the individual and the situation, we must be able to deter-mine how the individual was affected by the situation. Kennedy used Rusk primarily as an administrative officer.[35] In contrast, "President Johnson, forced by the Vietnam war to make more and more critical decisions in the area of foreign affairs, relied on Secretary Rusk much more consistently than had President Kennedy."[36] Hence, Rusk should have been more important under Johnson than he was under Kennedy. However, since Johnson surrounded himself with "yes" men, Rusk's position becomes slightly less clear—at best, ambiguous. Thus any evaluation of Rusk's attitudes and actions before and after Tet—unless they are obtained rigorously and comprehensively—is likely to be rather impressionistic and "nongeneralizable."

Clearly, even though the Tet offensive is less difficult for the standard types of political and foreign policy analyses than the other cases we have discussed, it is not completely amenable to the standard forms of research if the question is flexibility. The dramatic events of the months following Tet, although important, cannot be assumed to be indicative of all statements and actions during that period. It is clear, then, that neither the situation nor the individuals involved in it have been sufficiently examined to make a proper assessment of the flexibility—actual or potential—exhibited by the decision-makers.

The Middle East War: King Richard and His Metternich

Our final case is the 1973 Middle East war and the United States' reactions to it. The actors are Richard M. Nixon and Secretary of State Henry Kissinger. The 1973 war itself was different from the other conflicts that had erupted in this area since the end of World War II. It began on Yom Kippur and lasted the greater part of three weeks—when compared to the six-day war of 1967, it was long indeed. By the time a cease-fire was arranged, the Israelis had regained much of the territory they had lost in the Sinai. They had bombed Damascus and had complete control over the Golan Heights. The price they paid was a great loss of personnel and unclear battle lines in many areas. By the end of the war, peace had clearly to be negotiated, or the Middle East might again explode. Why, however, did the United States decide to send Henry Kissinger on a series of trips that have become known as shuttle diplomacy? Why did it fail to react more forcefully to the postwar oil embargo? Why did Nixon choose to emphasize the Sinai agreement as a great foreign policy achievement? Perhaps Gary S. Schiff gives an insight into this complex situation:

> The 1973 Arab-Israeli War was fundamentally and qualitatively different from its predecessors. In those differences lie the possibilities for a settlement to the Middle East conflict.
>
> For one, the outcome differed sharply from that of the preceding wars. This time there was no clear victor or vanquished; each side was able to claim victory for its own purposes. Thus, the vastly improved Arab performance has enabled Egypt . . . to overcome its long standing sense of military inferiority. . . . For the Israelis, the war, while once again showing their greater resourcefulness, nevertheless disabused them of the illusion of permanent military superiority. . . .
>
> The war also underscored for Israel the fundamental political and military roles of the outside Great Powers in the conflict. . . . Indeed, the Arabs' ability to accept the United States, until recently the chief "colonialist" supporter of Israel, as mediator is another important consequence of the war itself.[37]

However, there is a different view of the 1973 Middle East war. It centers not on the conflict itself but on its effects on the participants, Fouad Ajami argues: "Self-righteous arguments, diplomatic maneuvers, and the capacity to generate transnational support and tensions are . . . weapons used in the Middle East conflict. Another one, the oil weapon, has been recently added to the arsenal, with very serious implications and an impact that is yet to unfold."[38] Ajami further states that events in the Middle East confront the entire world with a crisis of perception: "The central question that has yet to be resolved in the Middle East, and in which people throughout the world, and Arabs and Israelis in particular, have a vested interest, can be simply put: Will the future prevail or will it be irresponsibly, nihilistically, and arrogantly sacrificed? Essentially, a survival-challenge is at the crux of the matter."[39]

If Ajami is correct, the Middle East situation was indeed a crisis and in some senses continues to be a crisis. If, indeed, the survival of the world is at stake, then the reactions of decision-makers such as Nixon and Kissinger are important not only in a heuristic sense but also in terms of the future of humanity. What, then, can we find out about these two very important men?

In the case of President Nixon, there appears to be more information available—even if the conclusions drawn from that information are more biased than in the cases of the other presidents. This may be due in large measure to President Nixon's uniqueness in being a nationally active political figure for well over twenty-five years. Moreover, his political demise was so dramatic as to capture the imagination of many writers; as a result, we are often treated to armchair analysis of Nixon's character, to explanations of his actions that may or may not be accurate. Jerry Voorhis describes Nixon as president:

> It was Richard Nixon who was pleased to dress the White House policemen in uniforms which would be appropriate only in an imperial court. On occasion his guards are said to address him as "Your Excellency." It is Richard Nixon who follows a monarchial custom and has religious services held for him . . . in his Executive Mansion instead of attending church with his fellow citizens. It is Richard Nixon who has travelled to many lands at taxpayer's expense—and almost always to lands ruled by men with monarchical power where ordered pomp and ceremony would greet him and where there was no danger that the voices of free people would mar the occasion. . . . But strangely he seldom visited nations having free speech and free assembly. . . . Once, too, the President went to Rome to

meet with the Pope of the Catholic Church. But no chances were taken with the Italian people. Instead the President arrived at the Vatican by helicopter, landing in St. Peter's Square.... Not only does the President like to visit foreign countries where some brand of dictatorship holds sway, he seems simply to like dictatorships. His preference for Yahya Khan over Mrs. Gandhi is now classic.[40]

If Voorhis's description of Nixon's attitude toward the accumulation and use of power is accurate, then we have a frightening sense that when faced with a crisis Richard M. Nixon would be likely to act in his own best interest, regardless of the effect on the populace. In addition, his decisions on policy would be made on the basis of subjective evidence. His decisions, then, are his interpretations of reality—as Nixon's own words indicate. Early in his presidential career, Nixon spoke to the UN General Assembly on world peace:

I have had the great privilege over the past twenty-three years to travel to most of the countries represented in this room. I have met most of the leaders of the nations represented in this room. And I have seen literally thousands of people in most of the countries represented in this room.... Based on my own experience, of this one thing I am sure: The people of the world, wherever they are, want peace.... Now, I realize that a survey of history might discourage those who seek to establish peace. But we have entered a new age ... for the first time ever, we have truly become a single world community. For the first time ever, technological advance has brought within reach what was once only a poignant dream ... freedom from hunger and want; want and hunger that I have personally seen in nation after nation all over the world.[41]

One wonders whether Nixon would be so concerned about hunger if he had not seen it himself. But the point remains that Nixon seems to view world peace and world hunger in terms only of his own experiences and ideas. If we then try to extrapolate from these statements enough evidence to give us some indication of Nixon's public reaction to the Middle East conflict, we are left with a difficult task. For if he was indeed monarchial, if he trusted only, or at least predominantly, his own experience, he would quite likely react to the situation in the Middle East with a great deal of pomp and circumstance and tend to support actions and policies of his own design based on his own needs—rather than seeing the situation as it really was.

What were Nixon's needs? Herein lies one of the difficulties with the traditional literature. Its writers are perspicacious, but very few provide the list of priorities needed to make the accurate predictions we wish to make in this context. For example, if the notion of dictatorship was most appealing to Nixon, one would expect him to support the socialist and monarchist Arabs over the democratic Israelis. This is at least partially true, in the sense that our foreign policy toward the Middle East under Nixon tended to become less pro-Israeli. However, Nixon made a career for himself by accusing his opponents of being communists or communist supporters. How, then, could he support socialistic countries that supported the Soviet Union and that were militarily and economically supported by the Soviet Union? Still another aspect of the problem is Nixon's supposed preference for operating in the area of foreign affairs (as all good monarchs are wont to do). One would therefore expect that the opportunity for prestige and glory during and after the war would be too great a temptation for Nixon and that he would become personally involved in the situation. Yet this was empirically not the case.[42] In fact, Nixon was dramatically less active in foreign policy after the Middle East war. One obvious explanation for this, and for the alleged engineering of the "energy crisis" after the war, is that Nixon was too involved in the Watergate affair to worry about foreign policy—except as a means to divert attention from his domestic problems. Yet if this were true, it would contradict the premise that we are now discussing and support the earlier premise that Nixon viewed the entire world through a single set of lenses. What was most important to Nixon was therefore most important for the world. To continue the logic, Nixon at the time viewed staying in office as the most important item on the agenda, and therefore the bulk of his time had to be spent protecting his position. It was logical, therefore, to ignore foreign affairs unless foreign affairs could help preserve his presidency.

This exercise in extended extrapolation and inference points out the difficulty in explaining the motives for Nixon's behavior (or lack of it) before and after the Middle East war. These explanations are at best suggestive. They are not hard evidence for conclusions about Nixon's attitudes on foreign policy in general or on the Middle East in particular.

Although none dare call him king, some would have us call Henry Kissinger a modern-day Metternich. Kissinger's role in the foreign policy process, his impact on major problems of the world, and his scholarly writing—all have been analyzed by many scholars. Our central interest is Kissinger's role in the Middle East and any information about his role in it.

In order to assess Kissinger's general role as secretary of state in foreign policy, it is necessary to compare his behavior and attitudes with the behavior and attitudes of previous secretaries of state. Gaddis Smith, who attempts to compare the secretaries of state since 1914 on the basis of fifteen variables, finds that four had "great personal influence" in foreign affairs.

> The four most influential Secretaries—Kissinger, Dulles, Acheson, Hughes—possessed in a high degree certain common characteristics which reinforced each other in a circular flow of power: authority granted by the President, bureaucratic power over rivals, diplomatic power with foreign leaders, attention from the press, and power of expression. With the exception of attention from the press, all of these elements were essential for influence. Remove any one and the other would collapse.[43]

The four variables Smith employs—namely, authority, bu-
reaucratic power, foreign power, and expressive power—seem
to be a definition of influence rather than an analysis of influence. In this sense, they are tautological. If we ignore this
criticism, however, we are left with the conclusion that
Kissinger was an influential secretary of state. Yet that alone
tells us little about Kissinger's role in the Middle East or the
impact his personality had on the situation. The question of
style then becomes crucial. There can be many styles, even
among influential secretaries, and the style becomes increas-
ingly important as the secretary becomes more influential. In
the case of Kissinger, who became secretary during a time of
unbridled executive power in foreign affairs, the question of
style and influence assumes even greater importance. How
one uses that power and the authority with which one assumes
that power has been described by Albert F. Eldridge, Jr:

> Sweeping and unilateral Presidential authority in foreign poli-
> cy making did not spring up full blown in the Nixon Presi-
> dency. . . . The President [Nixon] attempted to expand the
> war-making powers of his office into other areas of foreign
> policy. The Congress challenged these actions. Both campaigns
> met with mixed degrees of success depending upon the actor's
> perspectives. . . . Henry Kissinger's actions and beliefs have
> been both a stimulus and a response to these changing political
> and philosophical trends. He played a significant role in but-
> tressing presidential authority in foreign policy during the first
> Nixon administration. In the process he acquired for himself
> unprecedented political power, formal authority and public
> support. . . . One of the legacies of his preeminent power and
> authority . . . has been that he, rather than the President, has
> become the lightning rod of dissent over foreign policy.[44]

It seems a fair assumption, then, that Henry Kissinger used
the power granted to him for self-aggrandizement. Moreover,
Nixon's demise and Ford's passive leadership in foreign affairs created a situation in which Henry Kissinger was the

major, if not the sole, force in formulating foreign policy.

If this is so and if the process is one of the incremental growth of power, then it is fair to assume that at the time of the Middle East war, Kissinger already had great, if not superior, power. (This was the time of Watergate.) How Kissinger used this power becomes the next question.

Kissinger was at least partially successful in his efforts to negotiate a settlement in the Middle East. He did, in fact, achieve an Egyptian-Israeli disengagement in the Sinai. But was this diplomatic victory a Pyrrhic one? Some critics have claimed that the bilateral agreement Kissinger achieved actually lessened the probability of an overall Middle East peace.[45] Dana Ward offers a possible explanation not only for the behavior but also for the personality traits that could have led to this behavior:

> Another aspect of Kissinger's personality, with both defensive and adaptive characteristics, is the feeling that acceptance and goodness are earned. Here the drive to succeed would become important and is related to his capacity for work, but perhaps even more important are the interpersonal skills Kissinger would develop so that others would accept and trust him. . . .
> It seems clear to me that Kissinger's ideology, as well as his experience negotiating the peace agreement in Vietnam, made a major contribution to Kissinger's choice of tactics. Believing that one can not stem the tide of history, Kissinger believes that the best one can hope for is to slow its ebb, buy time, achieve a "decent interval." This was the tactic which led to the paper peace in Vietnam, and it appears that it has produced another paper peace in the Middle East. Rather than negotiating the truly difficult problems of the Golan Heights, the Palestinians, and Jerusalem, which undoubtedly would have took [sic] more time, required multilateral negotiations, and perhaps even a meeting of all parties involved, Kissinger chose instead his highly publicized shuttle diplomacy. . . .
> The second related psychological factor which contributed to Kissinger's choice of tactics in the Middle East is another

characteristic typical of the depressive personality: insatiability in status and glory.[46]

This last statement is reminiscent of George Ball's criticism of Kissinger, that is, Ball claims that Kissinger moved into the void created by a hamstrung Nixon in order to fulfill a need for power.[47]

Kissinger, therefore, can be viewed as a personality that must constantly seek new sources of power to add to his arsenal. This conclusion and the insights of various authors on the interplay of personality and situation come closer than any material cited for the other individuals in the study to the type of prediction we seek. But the very success in the case of Kissinger further illustrates the inability of scholars to be generally predictive. Without criticizing the validity of the findings, it can be shown that the predictive ability is valid for only one individual. No further generalization can be safely made.

Adding Apples, Oranges, and Bananas

This chapter began by maintaining that this research differs from other work on foreign policy not so much in the questions asked but in the procedures employed to provide answers to them. Almost all of the cases examined can be and have been subjected to differing interpretations. Moreover, motivations are virtually impossible to discern except by inference. It was not my purpose to provide an exhaustive historical account of each case or a biography of each individual. Rather, it was merely to demonstrate the variety of opinions that exist and the plethora of conclusions that can be drawn from one and the same set of facts.

No one study cited in this chapter is necessarily inaccurate. On balance, they are respected for their insights as well as the reporting of factual information. But each is interested in a different set of variables. Moreover, each starts with a different set of assumptions. Different assumptions lead to different research designs and—unfortunately for one who seeks to develop generalizations—to different conclusions.

Chapter 6 is an attempt to remedy all these problems. I shall report the results of the data collection and hypothesis testing free from the problems of data comparability. I examine the same variables for each individual, and by doing so I may be able to make general statements about the flexibility of various types of decision-makers.

Predicting Flexible Behavior

The research framework attempts to discern the flexibility that decision-makers will exhibit after they have experienced a crisis failure. This chapter presents the results. In addition, it reports patterns of behavior that were not discussed in the research design but that did emerge during data collection.

The Data Set: Advantages and Limitations

Before reporting the results of my hypothesis testing, it is necessary to describe in some detail the data set that has been collected. Any data set has strengths and weaknesses, a full knowledge of which is necessary if one is to make reliable and valid statements based upon it.

This data set was collected according to the coding rules established in the research design.[1] The coding of public speeches for each individual for each time period yielded a total of 308 coded units (most of which were complete speeches).[2] Each unit was coded for referents, goal themes, and policy themes.[3]

The major data source for the coding was the *New York Times*. Only when a speech or a news conference was *not* transcribed in full was the original testimony or transcript referred to.[4] In almost all cases, the *New York Times* provided enough information for purposes of coding. All speeches, public statements, testimony before committees, news conferences, and the like were identified for each of the individuals in the study from the *New York Times Index.* Only verbatim transcripts were coded, and those speeches and new conferences that referred to domestic affairs were not included in the sample. In the case of news conferences, a unit was considered to be a question or a series of questions that referred to a specific area of foreign policy. It was possible, therefore, that a news conference contained a number of questions about only one aspect of foreign policy or was related exclusively to certain domestic issues.[5] In these cases, it was decided to view all questions about the same area of interest or substantive issue as a single "unit" for purposes of coding.

The advantages of this method of data collection are: first, it provides a comparative sample across five crises and ten individuals;[6] second, the use of publicly available data allows any results obtained to be replicated for the individuals in the study and for other decision-makers outside the scope of the original research; third, an overall view of flexibility allows us to use the collected data for hypothesis generation and as an avenue to more detailed research in this area. The disadvantages of this approach to the collection of data for the discovery of mental sets and change in mental sets and behavior are also rather clear. This method does *not* attempt to explain the mechanism of the psychological filters themselves. No claim is made that public documents provide the most precise information that is available on all decision-makers. Moreover, I do not claim that the variables I have described are the most accurate predictors of the types of behavior change in which I am interested.

Each decision-maker in the current research was examined for two six-month periods: one before the crisis failure (pre-crisis) and a second after the crisis failure (post-crisis). Table 8 presents the frequencies of foreign policy–related speeches for each individual under analysis during each period.

TABLE 8

FREQUENCY OF FOREIGN POLICY RELATED SPEECHES

INDIVIDUAL	PRE-CRISIS	POST-CRISIS
Truman	13	7
Marshall	18	8
Eisenhower	21	20
Dulles	23	17
Kennedy	32	32
Rusk	13	12
Johnson	22	14
Rusk	8	5
Nixon	14	9
Kissinger	9	11

The pattern that emerges in Table 8 is quite interesting. Except for President Kennedy, who had the same number of codable speeches before and after the Berlin crisis, and Kissinger, who was not appointed secretary of state until after the beginning of the pre-crisis sample period, all individuals in the study exhibit less verbal behavior after the crisis than before the crisis. There are several possible explanations for this. Perhaps the decision-makers in question tended to be more cautious—after failure so as not to stumble into another failure or exacerbate what has already taken place. These findings may also indicate avoidance—the intentional or unintentional denial of the importance or reality of a certain class of situations. After failure, a decision-maker may well avoid the source of failure (foreign policy) and seek more successful areas of activity. Avoidance can also occur if the decision-maker denies responsibility for the initial failure but projects his difficulties onto another target (such as the media) and then avoids situations that are viewed as triggers for the target. For example, Kennedy may not have seen the Berlin crisis as a failure, or he may have had so much self-confidence and ego strength that the failure in no way affected his perception in foreign policy. More likely, Kennedy was more attracted to foreign policy than other presidents in the study and would deal with foreign policy more often *regardless* of the perceived risks. Kissinger's increase in activity after the Middle East war can be attributed to two factors. First, Kissinger was not appointed secretary until after the pre-crisis period began, and second, he became the prime mediator of the disengagement agreement during the post-crisis period. These findings are also supported by other research on crisis. Thus, Charles A. McClelland, while investigating the Quemoy and Berlin crises, discovered that during the period of "crisis abatement" the average of all types of behavior tends to be lower than the average of all behavior during the pre-crisis period.[7]

Measuring Flexibility

Before we can test any of the hypotheses suggested, we must determine how much the goals, policies, and themes of the decision-makers under study actually changed between the pre-crisis and post-crisis periods. This is essential since all of our hypotheses relate certain predictive variables to the degree of flexibility exhibited by a decision-maker.

Initially, I stated that three indicators of change were to be assessed. The most important of these is a change in goals (this indicates second-order change). The second most important is a change in policies. And the least important is a change in referents. Thus, before we can test our hypotheses relating predictive variables to change, we must describe any variation in the selected indicators.

Since the most important indicator is variation in goal theme, I will turn to this first. Goals can change in at least two ways: first, the *variety* of goals can change; second, the *frequency of appearance* of certain goals can change. Table 9

TABLE 9

GOAL DISTRIBUTION*

INDIVIDUAL	PRE-CRISIS GOAL	N	POST-CRISIS GOAL	N
Truman	World Peace	7	World Peace	6
	Resist Tyrants	4	Strengthen Democ-	5
	Feed Europe	3	racies	
			Strengthen Pres. in	1
			Foreign Policy	
Marshall	European Recovery	6	Resist Tyrants	4
	World Peace	5	World Peace	3
	Resist Tyrants	3	German Peace Treaty	1
	Support UN	3		
Eisenhower	World Peace	9	Increase Security	14
	Increase Security	9	World Peace	5
	Disarmament	3	Nuclear Test Ban	3
	Nuclear Test Ban	3		
Dulles	Stop Communism	9	Stop Communism	7
	World Peace	3	World Peace	4
	Disarmament	3	Disarmament	3
			Support Taiwan	3
Kennedy	"Freedom of Man"	9	Aid Latin America	7
	Increase Security	8	Increase Security	6
	Resist Communism	7	Nuclear Test Ban	5
Rusk	World Peace	3	S.E. Asian Peace	3
	S.E. Asian Peace	2	World Peace	2
	Support W. Germany	2	Eco. Cooperation	2
Johnson	Support Troops in	8	Seek Peace in Viet.	7
	Vietnam		World Peace	3
	Resist Communism	4	Support Troops in	3
	Increase Security	3	Vietnam	
Rusk	S.E. Asian Peace	4	S.E. Asian Peace	2
	World Peace	1	World Peace	1
	Prevent Nuclear War	1	Seek Nigerian Peace	1
Nixon	World Peace	6	Middle East Peace	3
	New World Order	2	World Peace	3
Kissinger	World Peace	3	Middle East Peace	5
	SALT Agreement	3	National Interest	1
	Seek Just World	2		

* Only the three goals which appear most
frequently for each individual are included
in this table.

summarizes the goals articulated by each individual under
study and the frequency with which each goal appears both
before and after the crisis failure.

What goal change or lack of change did each decision-maker exhibit? Before the Czechoslovak coup, Truman's primary goal was the construction of a lasting "world peace," a goal theme that he articulated seven times during that period (a total of twenty-four goal themes were recorded for Truman during this period). After the Czechoslovak coup, Truman's most dominant goal theme remained "world peace," which appeared 50 percent of the time. But a second goal theme—that of "strengthening of democracies against communist attack"—accounted for 42 percent of the themes. This second goal was perhaps a reaction to events in Europe, and when taken together, the two goals may reflect a hardening of Truman's determination to resist Soviet domination of Eastern Europe even if such resistance might be somewhat contradictory to the goal of world peace.

Much the same is evident in the goals expressed by Secretary of State Marshall. During the first period, two goals dominated his statements: "world peace" and "European recovery." In the post-crisis period, "world peace" remained, but "European recovery" was replaced by "resistance to tyrants," a theme that is quite similar to Truman's theme of "strengthening democracies against communist attacks."

It is also evident that during the pre-crisis period, both Truman and Marshall articulated goals that were broader both in terms of geography and subject matter. In the post-crisis period, they narrowed their focus to peace and security issues. This can be seen as a turning point in the evolution of the Cold War between the United States and the Soviet Union.[8] A mere narrowing of goals is not necessarily positive or negative in a normative sense; rather, this particular narrowing tends to confirm the view that during the late 1940s attitudes and perceptions of foreign policy changed. From that point on, many if not all events were viewed as having an impact upon the relations between the United States and the Soviet Union.

In the Eisenhower administration, by contrast, change was so minor as to be merely a statistical artifact rather than a significant finding. Both President Eisenhower and Secretary of State Dulles exhibited little change in the goals that seemed most important to them, "world peace" and "containing world communism." Before the Lebanese crisis, Eisenhower mentioned the goals of "world peace" and "increasing security against the Russians" nine times each. Each theme accounts for 33 percent of his goal themes, or 66 percent of all the goals Eisenhower mentioned during the pre-crisis period. After the Lebanese crisis, these same goals were again ranked first and second. The only change was that the security issue had begun to overshadow the issue of peace. In the post-crisis period, the security goal accounted for 45 percent of the total and the goal of world peace, 15.6 percent.

Dulles is a study in the expected. Our findings tend to support other research on Eisenhower's secretary of state.[9] In the pre-crisis period, Dulles's principal goal was "stopping communism," and in the post-crisis period, the same goal also appeared most frequently. This overarching goal accounted for 40 percent of Dulles's goals in the pre-crisis period and 33 percent of them in the post-crisis period. It may be argued that even this small change in percentage of appearance can be explained by the fact that Dulles made fewer speeches during the post-crisis period, owing in large measure to his illness.

The Kennedy administration is rather puzzling. The Berlin crisis occurred early during the Kennedy presidency but following another foreign policy fiasco, the "Bay of Pigs." If one were to look only at the most prevalent goal, Kennedy's goals seemingly changed dramatically from the pre-Berlin to the post-Berlin period. During the pre-crisis period, Kennedy's dominant goal was the "freedom of man"; in the post-crisis period, his dominant goal was the desire to help the "countries of Latin America." This change in goals, however, must be examined more closely if we are to have confidence in the finding. If one looks at the leading four goals during each period, the type of change noted is just as dramatic if not more so than the one first mentioned. During the pre-crisis period, Kennedy's goals in order of frequency were (1) "freedom of man," (2) "United States security," (3) "resistance to communism," and (4) "support for European integration." After Berlin, his top four goals were (1) "assistance to Latin America," (2) "United States security," (3) "support for a nuclear test ban treaty," and (4) "seeking a lasting peace."

The differences among these goals are dramatic, and the significance of such a change needs to be discussed. During the post-crisis period, Kennedy seemingly became much more specific in the goals he sought to achieve. The general goals of "freedom of man" and "resistance to communism" gave way to the more specific and tangible goals of a test ban treaty and aid to Latin America. Perhaps Kennedy realized that idealistic pronouncements may create a fine spirit, but that a fine spirit alone does not necessarily solve problems. If the goal called "United States security" can be considered a role-oriented goal, then the change in goals exhibited by Kennedy becomes even more dramatic. (Role-oriented goals are goals that are usually attached to a certain office. Thus one of a police chief's goals is normally the peace and order of his town. This goal tends to be role-oriented.)

In contrast to Kennedy, Rusk stands out as a decision-maker of "quiet" ways. Rusk's marginal role in the Kennedy administration and his lack of public statements before and after Berlin makes a determination of goal change rather difficult. During the first period, he articulated only twelve goal themes, and during the post-Berlin period, only eleven goal themes. Rusk's reticence makes generalizations difficult, especially since the highest frequency for any goal theme in either period was three. Even so, three themes do appear more than once in both periods. In the first, the three goals that appear most frequently are (1) "seeking peace," (2) "Southeast Asian peace and security," and (3) "strengthening of Western commitment to Berlin and West Germany."

In the second period, the goals were (1) "Southeast Asian peace and security," (2) "seeking peace," and (3) "economic cooperation with the other nations of the world." These differences do indicate some change, but the small number forces us to be rather skeptical of this seeming change.

If we must be careful about the results of goal theme change for Secretary Rusk under President Kennedy, there is no reason at all to be skeptical about the results of goal coding for Rusk's second commander in chief, Lyndon B. Johnson. The change in goals from pre-crisis to post-crisis for Johnson was indeed dramatic: it was not merely a change in frequency of an articulated goal but the articulation of a *novel* goal, which then predominated after Tet. Before Tet, Johnson's dominant goal was the search for increased support of United States and allied troops in Vietnam. This goal accounted for 32 percent of Johnson's total goals and was followed by the corollary goal of "resistance to communism," which appeared 14 percent of the time. In marked contrast, the search for a negotiated peace in Vietnam became the dominant goal during the second period, appearing 50 percent of the time.

Rusk, on the other hand, tended to become even more silent than he had been under Kennedy, making it, as ever, difficult to generalize about his goals. Indeed, he tended to express goal themes even less often under Johnson than he had under Kennedy. During the Johnson administration, Rusk showed a remarkable capacity to issue statements and make speeches that contained referents and policy themes but no goal themes. Based on what little information we have been able to obtain, Rusk's dominant goal theme for both periods was "Southeast Asian peace." This goal appeared three times in the pre-crisis period and only twice in the post-crisis period.

President Richard M. Nixon, the final chief executive under study, exhibited considerable goal change. Before the Middle East war, he consistently emphasized "world peace"

(54.5 percent). After the Middle East war, the goal of "world peace" (27.2 percent) shared preeminence with the more specific goal of "Middle East peace" (27.2 percent). Nixon clearly had changed his goals—both in terms of frequency and in terms of scope.

Henry Kissinger exhibited goal changes not unlike those exhibited by President Nixon. Before the Middle East war, the most important goals for Kissinger were "world peace" and the "SALT talks." After the Middle East war, the dominant goal was the achievement of "peace in the Middle East." This does not seem to be a dramatic change, but the category that increased most dramatically was not a specific goal but rather a lack of goal. Like Rusk under Johnson, Kissinger during the post-crisis period demonstrated an ability to issue statements and make speeches without saying anything about his goals. Perhaps it is Kissinger's style of negotiation, or perhaps the arrangements he was making for a Middle East peace were so delicate that he could not express his goals. However we interpret it, the fact remains that Kissinger made statements without goals much more often during the post-crisis period than anyone else except Rusk.

The second most important indicator of change is policy theme. A decision-maker may well mention more than one policy theme in a speech. Since the unit of analysis is the decision-maker himself, it is then necessary to calculate an overall score for each decision-maker for the pre-crisis and post-crisis periods. These scores are based on a weighting system that gives a weight of +3 to cooperative deed behavior, +2 to cooperative word behavior, -2 to conflictful word behavior, and -3 to conflictful deed behavior and then adds the number of participant activity.[10] All scores can thus vary from a +3 to a -3. As Table 10 indicates, for example, President Truman's mean pre-crisis behavior was +1.95. This statistic indicates that his behavior tended toward *verbal* behavior of *cooperative* affect. During the post-Czechoslovak period, Truman's behavior score was +1.16, lower than during

TABLE 10

WEIGHTED POLICY THEMES

INDIVIDUAL	PRE-CRISIS	POST-CRISIS	DIFFERENCE
Truman	1.95	1.16	.79
Marshall	.70	.72	.02
Eisenhower	1.18	1.47	.29
Dulles	.42	.86	.44
Kennedy	1.49	1.11	.38
Rusk	.60	.58	.02*
Johnson	.70	1.07	.37
Rusk	.43	2.00	1.57*
Nixon	1.35	1.83	.48
Kissinger	.90	.63	.26

*The figures for policy theme for Rusk are based on an "n" of 15 and 7. This "n" may be too small to make substantive judgements and therefore the figures for Rusk are being dropped from the rank order correlations.

the first period. This difference may reflect a change from a more activist to a less activist overall behavior profile, since the score of +1.16 is much closer to participant activity than to cooperative verbal behavior. In addition to the weighted policy theme scores for each period, the last column of Table 10 gives the differences between the two periods. The statistic will serve as the basis for further discussion of change in terms of our hypothesis.

The weakest indicator of change is a change in referent but no change of goal theme and policy theme. Such change may merely indicate a variation in rhetoric or audience rather than a significant alteration in foreign policy behavior. Referents are classified along three dimensions: temporal, spatial, and affectual. Since there are not enough data to discuss affectual referents and since all the decision-makers in the sample used a predominance of foreign referents (the smallest percentage being 66.7 percent for Truman), only the temporal dimension of referents will be discussed in detail. Table 11 summarizes the percentage of each type of referent for each period and gives the differences among the types overall. As Table 11 reveals, most decision-makers did exhibit some change in referents between the pre-crisis and post-crisis periods. Not unexpectedly in light of our other indicators of change, Secretary of State Dulles exhibited the least change even in terms of referent—no category more than a 0.5 percent change. At the highest levels, changes of 32.7 percent were recorded for Truman. Again we see that Dulles tended to pursue the same goals, policies, and even referents before and after his crisis failure.

We have thus far discussed the three indicators of change and have presented the degrees of change that each decision-maker has exhibited according to each indicator. We know, however, that not all indicators are of equal importance in terms of flexibility. To reflect this fact, we have created an artificial and synthetic system that assigns utilities to the various indicators of change. By assigning a weight of 5 to changes in goals, a weight of 3 to changes in policy and a weight of 1 to changes in referent, one converts nominal to a more ordinal form. In a sense, we are subjectively assigning values to preferences, and in the process we are making the different types of change more easily comparable. Table 12 summarizes these indicators in a way that will facilitate comparison. The following rules were used to assign the various weights. Any decision-maker who exhibited any change in goals that corresponded to the results given in Table 9 was assigned a value of 5. Any decision-maker who exhibited a change in policy theme of over 0.30 was considered to have changed policy and was assigned a value of 3. Finally, any decision-maker who exhibited a 5 percent change in referents was assigned a value of 1. Table 12 also contains the overall

TABLE 11

TEMPORAL REFERENT CHANGE OVERALL

INDIVIDUAL	PRE-CRISIS				POST-CRISIS				CHANGE		
	N	Past	Pres	Fut	N	Past	Pres	Fut	Past	Pres	Fut
Truman	38	47.3	44.7	7.9	15	80.0	20.0	0.0	32.7	24.7	7.9
Marshall	36	30.5	61.1	8.3	19	63.0	36.8	0.0	32.5	24.3	8.3
Eisenhower	41	68.3	29.2	2.4	44	61.3	36.3	2.2	7.0	7.1	0.2
Dulles	37	59.4	40.5	0.0	39	58.9	41.0	0.0	0.5	0.5	0.0
Kennedy	77	41.5	50.6	7.8	53	32.0	62.2	5.6	9.5	11.6	2.2
Rusk	27	44.4	51.8	3.7	20	20.0	80.0	0.0	24.4	28.2	3.7
Johnson	43	44.1	51.1	4.6	63	41.2	55.5	3.1	2.9	4.4	1.5
Rusk	11	18.2	72.7	9.1	8	62.5	37.5	0.0	44.3	35.2	9.1
Nixon	22	36.3	59.1	4.5	21	42.8	47.6	9.5	6.5	11.5	5.0
Kissinger	25	52.0	36.0	12.0	9	0.0	100.0	0.0	52.0	64.0	12.0

TABLE 12

OVERALL CHANGE

INDIVIDUAL	GOAL CHANGE	POLICY CHANGE	REFERENT CHANGE	TOTAL
Truman	3*	3	1	7
Marshall	5	0	1	6
Eisenhower	0	0	1	1
Dulles	0	3	0	3
Kennedy	5	3	1	9
Rusk	NA	NA	1	1
Johnson	5	3	1	9
Rusk	NA	NA	1	1
Nixon	5	3	1	9
Kissinger	0	0	1	1

*Truman is assigned a weight of 3 for for goal since he exhibited some change.

score for each decision-maker in terms of overall weighted change.

Referents as a Predictive Variable of Flexibility

Having described the change exhibited by each decision-maker over the sample periods, the next step is to assess the success with which the hypothesized predictive variables do in fact predict flexibility.

The first of these predictive variables is the referents that the decision-maker has used during the pre-crisis period. Recall the first general hypothesis:

I.   The greater the congruence between referent and the current situation, the greater the flexibility that will be exhibited.

This general hypothesis can be divided into several more discreet hypotheses, each referring to a different type of referent. Since, as already indicated, the spatial dimension of referents is so skewed toward foreign as to make any discussion of the hypotheses based on a foreign-domestic dichotomy useless, we are left with a discussion and test of those hypotheses that relate to temporal referents. Of the six remaining hypotheses, two are directly testable:

I-1. Leaders who use present foreign referents will tend to be the most flexible.

I-2. Leaders who use more past foreign referents will be only slightly more flexible than leaders who use past domestic referents. Leaders who use more past domestic referents will tend to be the least flexible.

In order to test these hypotheses, we must be able to determine which decision-maker exhibited more of the type of referents we are interested in examining. Two possible methods can be employed to determine each decision-maker's dominant referent type. The first examines each codable unit to determine the *modal referent type.* In case of a tie, both modal referents are entered into the aggregate of modal types. In the second method, each referent is treated as a data point *regardless* of whether it appears in the same speech as another referent. The dominant referent type is then determined by taking the mean of referent types for the entire pre-crisis period. If the decision-maker is the unit of analysis, the latter method seems the most appropriate, since the speech itself is "accidental" to the number and distribution of referents.

Although for most of the individuals involved, the modal and the overall dominant referent types do not differ, in certain cases they do. Perhaps the most obvious example is Secretary of State John Foster Dulles. According to the modal scores, Dulles used more present foreign referents than

TABLE 13

REFERENT PERCENTAGES

INDIVIDUAL	N	P	PR	FUT	N	FR	DOM
Truman	38	47.3	44.7	7.9	30	66.7	33.3
Marshall	36	30.5	61.1	8.3	36	91.6	8.3
Eisenhower	41	68.3	29.2	2.4	36	91.6	8.3
Dulles	37	59.4	40.5	0.0	37	86.4	13.5
Kennedy	77	41.5	50.6	7.8	81	88.8	11.1
Rusk	27	44.4	51.8	3.7	27	96.2	3.7
Johnson	43	44.1	51.1	4.6	43	81.3	18.6
Rusk	11	18.2	72.7	9.1	11	72.7	27.2
Nixon	22	36.3	59.1	4.5	24	70.8	29.2
Kissinger	25	52.0	36.0	12.0	24	83.3	16.6

P = Past   FUT= Future   FR = Foreign
PR = Present   DOM = Domestic

future or past ones. When we look at the overall totals, however, we discover that of all the referents Dulles used, only 40.5 percent were present, and 49.9 percent were past. This difference is due to the fact that many of the past referents were clustered together in "major speeches" and the present referents tended to be scattered throughout minor statements, thus skewing the sample to some degree. Since we have decided that the decision-maker rather than the speech is the unit of analysis for this purpose, it is necessary to use the overall percentages figures rather than the modal scores. The distribution of temporal and spacial referents is given in Table 13. These percentages will be used to distinguish between decision-makers who use more or less of a particular type of referent.

There are two procedures to test the hypotheses that we

TABLE 14

GOAL CHANGES AND PERCENTAGE OF REFERENTS

INDIVIDUAL	GOAL	% PRES	% PAST
Rusk 2	NA	72.7	18.2
Marshall	C	61.1	30.5
Nixon	C	59.1	36.3
Rusk 1	NA	51.1	44.4
Johnson	C	51.1	44.1
Kennedy	C	50.6	41.5
Truman	SC	44.7	47.3
Dulles	NC	40.5	59.4
Kissinger	NA	36.0	52.0
Eisenhower	NC	29.2	68.3

Rusk 1 = Rusk-Kennedy   NA = Not Applicable
Rusk 2 = Rusk-Johnson   C = Change
                                         SC = Some Change
                                         NC = No Change

have cited. The first is to examine each element of flexible behavior separately; the second, to compare overall change with the rank-order of certain types of referents. We shall first examine the relationship between past and present referents and the various types of changes individually. Table 14 compares the change in goals with the rank-order of past and present referents, respectively. We would expect a positive relationship between present referents and goal and a negative relationship between past referents and goal change. As reflected in Table 14, there is a positive correlation between the percentage of present referents and change in goals and a negative correlation between past referents and goal change. This supports the most important element in our test; since a change in goal theme reflects a change in the second-order purposes, this change stands out as the most important relationship about which we hypothesized.

The second most important indicator of change and flexibility is policy change. In order to test how well referents can predict for policy themes, we will use the differences in weighted policy behavior between pre-crisis and post-crisis periods as reported in Table 10. These data were rank-ordered and compared with the rank-orders of past and present referents. According to our hypothesis, there should be a positive relationship between present referents and change in policy theme and a negative relationship between past referents and policy themes. The rank-order correlation between present referents and policy theme change is 0.41, and the correlation between past referents and policy themes is 0.047.[11] In the first case it is easy to see how the hypothesis is supported.

In the second case, our hypothesis would have been more clearly supported if the correlation were negative. But the correlation itself is sufficiently close to zero to indicate that no relationship exists between past referents and policy change. In a technical sense, however, this finding still tends to support our hypothesis. The hypothesis does not state that past referents will be negatively related to flexibility but rather that past referents will be less positively related than present referents. In this sense, our hypothesis has been supported, albeit minimally.

The least important indicator of flexibility is a change in referents between the pre-crisis and post-crisis periods. Since all decision-makers except Dulles did exhibit some type of change in referents, one valid test of the hypothesis involves the calculation of two rank-order correlations: the first between the past referents and the degree of change overall and the second between the present referents and overall change in referents. The rank-order correlations are +0.49 and -0.45, respectively. Our hypothesis is again supported, both for the positive relationship between present referents and flexibility and for the negative relationship between past referents and flexibility.

In conclusion, we find that taken individually, all indicators of change are related positively to present referents and are negatively related or not related to past referents. Unfortunately, there are not enough data to test hypotheses on future and spatial referents and flexibility in a similar fashion.

A final test of hypothesis I is to compare the overall flexibility score (see Table 12) with the rank-ordering of past and present referents. The rank-order correlation between past referent and overall change is +0.16, and the rank-order correlation between present referents and overall change is a robust +0.74. In short, hypothesis I, which suggests that present referents are predictive of flexibility, is supported. Hypothesis I-2, which states that past referents are less strongly related to flexibility, is also supported.

Congruence as a Predictor of Flexibility

In addition to the predictive value of referents, I hypothesized that another predictor of flexible behavior is a measure I call congruence. Congruence is a measure of the "fit" along six dimensions of referents and goals during the pre-crisis period. The closer the "fit" (that is, the greater the agreement between referent and goal theme in terms of the six variables), the greater the likelihood that the decision-maker in question will exhibit flexible behavior.

In order to test this hypothesis, I have employed procedures quite similar to those used to test the hypotheses that related referents to flexibility. First, we must determine which decision-makers exhibited what degree of congruence, and then we must compare the results with our indicators of change, both singly and taken as a group. Congruence, like referents themselves, can be calculated in two ways for each individual in the study. The first procedure assumes the speech as the unit of analysis, determines a modal congruence score for each speech, and then uses a mean of the modal scores for an overall figure for each individual. The alternative procedure views the individual decision-maker as the unit of analysis and simply averages (means) all the congruence scores for the entire pre-crisis period. The latter procedure corresponds more closely to the assumptions inherent in the research design and will therefore be used to test the hypothesis. We shall use overall congruence scores to test the hypothesis by first comparing the ranks according to congruence with the degree to which each decision-maker exhibited change in goals between pre-crisis and post-crisis periods. Table 15 reflects this comparison.

The results presented in Table 15 reflect a somewhat mixed picture of the relationship between congruence and goal change. Although it can be argued that, on balance, there is some relationship between higher congruence scores and goal change, the appearance of Dulles at a fairly high congruence level but with no change in goals makes one less confident in the result than would otherwise be the case. A secondary test of this hypothesis of change is a rank-order correlation in which all those exhibiting change are classified in the top position, Truman in the middle, and those who exhibited no change in the bottom position. The result of this calculation is a strong correlation of 0.62. This high positive correlation supports the hypothesis and at the same time makes the case of Dulles appear more of an anomaly than one would conclude by simply scanning the data.

The second type of change that we wish to examine in light of our congruence predictor is that of policy theme. Again, the procedure used to determine a rank-order correlation between the change in policy theme is the rank-order correlation between congruence and policy theme. This calculation yields a correlation of 0.155. This result does *not*

TABLE 15

CONGRUENCE AND GOAL CHANGE

INDIVIDUAL	CONGRUENCE	GOAL CHANGE
Kennedy	.86	C
Johnson	.82	C
Nixon	.80	C
Dulles	.79	NC
Truman	.78	SC
Marshall	.77	C
Rusk 2	.77	NA
Kissinger	.74	NA
Rusk 1	.73	NA
Eisenhower	.66	NC

Rusk 1 = Rusk-Kennedy   NA = Not Applicable
Rusk 2 = Rusk-Johnson   C = Change
                              SC = Some Change
                              NC = No Change

support our hypothesis. However, the relationship is positive, even if minimally so.

The last type of change to be examined individually is change in referent. The procedure is again the rank-ordering of congruence with that of change in referents and then a calculation of a further rank-order correlation. This calculation yields a correlation of -0.43. This result is directly contrary to the result posited and the hypothesis. The negative relationship between congruence and referent change is difficult to explain, since referent change, in addition to being the least important indicator of flexibility, tends to mirror changes in goals and policies rather than precede them. Before claiming that the hypothesis on congruence has been supported, it is necessary to compare congruence scores with overall change in goals, policies, and referents. Again the ranking for this combined measure is in Table 12. The result of the rank-order correlation is +0.798. This is a very suggestive finding. It seems that congruence may be as good and even slightly better at predicting overall flexibility than present referent, even though present referents are better predictors of any one dimension of change. We could speculate at great length on why this relationship exists, but the data tend to support only the most general statements. A great deal more research would be necessary to determine the precise cause of this disparity in our findings. On balance, however, since our initial purpose was to discover and predict flexibility in a most general way, we must regard the hypotheses as supported.

Having supported the general hypotheses on congruence, we must now turn to the several subhypotheses that make up the general hypothesis. These subhypotheses relate the specific type of congruence to the degree of flexibility that is likely to be exhibited. Unfortunately, the data are not rich enough to test these hypotheses, since there is insufficient overlap between decision-makers in the individual variables that constitute the congruence measure to make such a test valid and reliable. This is unfortunate, but since the general hypothesis has been so convincingly supported, this gap in the data does not affect the overall impact of our results. Our third general hypothesis is:

III.   There is no relationship between foreign policy behavior and the presence of negative feedback.

This hypothesis and its progeny, which states that there will be no difference between foreign policy behavior before and after crisis failure, have already been disconfirmed. In short, we have disproved the null hypothesis, leading us to believe that the framework that was originally suggested is a viable method to analyze the behavior of individual decision-makers.

The final general hypothesis related the specificity of the crisis to a leader's ability to change goals and policies after a crisis. This hypothesis suggests that if a leader exhibits no other type of change, he will very likely change goals and policies in areas related to the subject matter of the crisis failure. In a sense, this hypothesis is now irrelevant: the hypotheses concerned with overall change have been supported. However, the data have revealed that the hypothesis can be supported at least by illustration. President Johnson is an excellent example of the type of specificity suggested in the hypothesis. Before Tet, Johnson's principal goal was related to Vietnam and support for the United States and allied troops in Southeast Asia. After Tet, his focus did not change, but his goal did. He now wished to negotiate a peace and get the problem behind him. Since Vietnam contributed greatly to Johnson's decision not to seek another term as president, one gets a picture of a foreign policy failure overshadowing an entire administration in the same way that Watergate overshadowed the Nixon administration and led ultimately to Nixon's resignation. Regardless of the insight that one can gain from the Johnson case, it is still difficult to test the hypotheses related to general hypothesis IV with the data that have been collected. This shortcoming is more than compensated for, however, when one realizes that the more general hypotheses have been supported.

This chapter has systematically presented the results of the data collection and analysis. The data collected have tended to support the hypotheses drawn from our theoretical framework. In general, whatever hypotheses could be tested were supported. All other hypotheses could not be tested owing to a paucity of data. Several findings suggest the need for further refinements in the framework and for new hypotheses that can be tested.

7

The Outcomes of Future Crises:
A Modest Prediction

At the heart of this study is the desire to develop a predictive model. The entire research design and the research on past administrations has been undertaken in order to test a series of hypotheses, which if supported, would enable a student of foreign policy to predict the behavior of current and future presidents and secretaries of state. This chapter analyzes President Jimmy Carter and Secretary of State Cyrus Vance.

This chapter offers predictions for both Carter and Vance if they experience a foreign policy crisis, especially one that might be considered a failure. The predictions made here are not predictions of specific behaviors but rather attempts to determine the types of behavior that they are likely to exhibit.

The Peanut Farmer and His Secretary

James Earl (Jimmy) Carter was elected president without the typical political career. He was born on October 1, 1924, in Plains, Georgia. That fact alone makes his election somewhat unique in the modern era, since the United States has not elected a Southern president as a rule (the only exception is Texas's Lyndon Johnson).

Carter's boyhood was spent in southwest Georgia and revolved around farming and the typical boyhood pleasures

of a rural area, including hunting and fishing. After his gradu-
ation (at the head of his class) from high school, he spent a
year in junior college, a year in Georgia Tech., and then went
on to the United States Naval Academy.

Carter graduated from Annapolis in 1947 and spent six
years in the navy before returning to Georgia to take over the
family business after the death of his father. Later, he
entered politics—first as a member of the Georgia legislature,
and then as governor of Georgia. After his term as Georgia's
chief executive, he began seriously to consider running for
president.

Many people can find traits in Carter's personality upon
which to base a prediction about his behavior as president.
Analogies abound, but there are few hard data upon which to
make predictions. Some people would argue that Carter's
deeply held religious beliefs might tend to make him
dogmatic and uncompromising—just as John Foster Dulles
was dogmatic and uncompromising.

Given his rural southern background, Carter also may be
quite provincial in his perceptions, and thus ill-informed and
unsophisticated about world affairs. As a result, Carter would
quite likely not deal with international relations if he could
avoid it; if he could not, his decisions and behaviors would be
inconsistent with the problems at hand, leading to an inef-
fective foreign policy.

Still another line of reasoning would suggest that given
Carter's high moral tone, his foreign policy is likely to be a
failure—because he will allow his moral beliefs to color his
view of the world. This high moral standard will probably
make Carter see the international scene as a series of black-
and-white choices rather than as a complex set of interwoven
issues. As a result, his foreign policy is likely to resemble that
of Woodrow Wilson more than any other president. This
moralistic foreign policy is likely to weaken the United
States' position globally, since decisions will be made on the
basis of what is morally acceptable rather than on realistic

considerations.

It should be emphasized that all the predictions for Carter based on these personality traits are impressionistic, nonrigorous, and rather unscientific. As we will see, the predictive model used seems to indicate that all the logical analogies drawn are somewhat incomplete, rather basic, and may in the long run be quite inaccurate. Before discussing those predictions, however, it would be helpful to examine rather briefly the background of the current secretary of state.

Cyrus Roberts Vance is as much a Washington insider as President Carter is a Washington outsider. Vance has now been appointed by three presidents to high federal positions. He has had several positions in the Defense Department and was a troubleshooter for President Johnson before President Carter appointed him secretary of state.

Born in Clarksburg, West Virginia, on March 27, 1917, Vance received his undergraduate degree in economics from Yale and then went on to Yale Law School. In 1942 he graduated from Yale and spent the rest of World War II in the navy. In 1947 he joined a New York law firm and remained there until 1957. In that year he went to Washington to help set up a Senate inquiry on military and space preparedness. His work came to the attention of the then Senate majority leader, Lyndon Johnson, who persuaded Vance to stay in Washington as the counsel for the Senate Preparedness Subcommittee.

With the election of John Kennedy in 1961, Vance was appointed the Defense Department's general counsel. From that point, his career in the Defense Department began to move ahead quickly. In 1962 President Kennedy appointed him secretary of the army, and in 1964 President Johnson made him deputy secretary of defense, the second highest civilian position in the department.

Vance performed his duties quite well but was forced to resign from his post as the result of a back injury compounded by difficulty with his knee. After his resignation, he returned to his New York law firm, but his government career was far from over. President Johnson called on him several times for special missions. This role was not a new one for Vance, since during his tenure at the Department of Defense, President Johnson sent him to the Panama Canal Zone during the riots of 1964 and to the Dominican Republic during the civil war of 1965. President Johnson also sent him to three trouble spots in 1967: South Vietnam (while still with the Defense Department), Detroit to observe the riots, and to the Mediterranean as a presidential troubleshooter to assist in the dispute over Cyprus.

Given his experience, Vance should be able to handle crises well. His government career should also help him deal with Congress and world leaders. Whether Vance is likely to take flexible stands on new crises, however, is unclear. His experience may have taught him to think on his feet and to be open to new alternatives. Or he may try to resolve new crises by using old solutions regardless of the similarity between the old and the new.

In short, both Carter and Vance are unknown entities in terms of foreign policy. Their general biographies and their career patterns suggest a number of possibilities rather than a predictive trend. By applying the model discussed earlier, it is hoped that predictions may be possible for the current foreign policy leadership.

Predictions for Carter and Vance

Carter's and Vance's public statements were analyzed for a six-month period beginning in January 1977 according to the rules set down for the other administrations we have studied. Using the procedures already established, 38 codable units were discovered for Carter and 15 for Vance. These units translate into 101 codable referents for Carter and 32 for Vance.

On the basis of frequencies alone, it is easy to see that both individuals fall into a familiar pattern of behavior.

Carter has made more speeches than other presidents, the closest being President Kennedy with thirty-two. This increase in the number of foreign policy–related statements over other chief executives is probably attributable to Carter's bimonthly news conferences and the fact that at the beginning of an administration a president may wish to state his overall foreign policy. Mr. Vance made fifteen speeches or responses, which gives him third place among the other secretaries of state. Dulles had the largest frequency (twenty-three), then Marshall (eighteen), and then Vance.

Frequencies alone, however, are not the basis of predictions. They are included merely to suggest that the coding scheme tends to produce rather expected results over time. The basis of prediction is the distribution of referents and the degree of congruence exhibited by these individuals. For both Carter and Vance, the pattern is typical of all the presidents and secretaries of state who have been examined. For example, Carter uses foreign referents 91.1 percent of the time, and Vance did not use anything but foreign referents. In addition, positive and negative referents were so infrequent that the calculation of percentages would be misleading. Thus, the main predictive tool for both Carter and Vance was the temporal distribution of referents.

Carter used present referents 68.3 percent of the time and Vance 53.3 percent. Carter thus ranked second behind Dean Rusk (during the Johnson administration) and Vance fifth, immediately after Nixon. Hence, we can easily conclude that Carter and Vance are likely to be rather flexible in most foreign policy areas. All the other individuals in this range of present referents were able to change goals and policies when faced with crisis failures, and the logic of the situation suggests that both Carter and Vance are rather likely to exhibit similar types of behavior.

Judging by present referents, it also seems logical to assert that neither Carter nor Vance is locked into past foreign policy situations and decisions. This might suggest, in a somewhat more speculative way, that in most foreign policy issue areas Carter and Vance are likely to be more flexible. This prediction requires that we push the framework to the limit, since it was designed to measure the potential for flexibility in high negative feedback situations. The pattern that emerges over most of the cases indicates that flexibility may also take place in non-crisis situations; the greater the percentage of present referents, the greater the flexibility in all situations—thus the prediction for Carter and Vance.

One other point needs to be made about referents. This analysis began by suggesting that referents could be measured along three dimensions—temporal, spacial, and affectual. As the research has indicated, the temporal dimension seems to show the most variation and is the most predictive for presidents and secretaries of state. The logical question, then, is whether the spacial and affectual dimensions have any utility for predicting flexibility.

At least two responses can be made to this question. First, these dimensions do exist and are important in general; but when dealing with the president and his secretary of state, they are less important than they would be if other decision-makers were being studied. Second, although these other dimensions of referents do exist, they are very weak predictors of flexibility.

Although it is difficult to choose either alternative until the scope of this type of study is widened, the first alternative has more appeal for several reasons. First, there was variation in spacial referents, but this variation was rather small. This does not mean that if we examined the president's political advisors for their foreign policy behaviors, we would not find a much wider variation in spacial referents, which would in turn have a large impact on their foreign policy flexibility. Second, affectual referents have not been as frequent as either temporal or spacial referents, but that does not mean they are unimportant or that they will not prove to be valuable predictors in future studies. In short, until a broader research effort is made, it is not possible to determine the utility of the other two dimensions of referent. At this point it would be better not to discard them until the evidence is obtained.

Another way to predict the behavior of Carter and Vance is to examine their overall congruence scores and compare these scores with those of the other individuals in the study. Overall congruence scores are poor predictors of any single dimension of change but are the best predictors of overall change. The overall congruence score for Carter is 0.85 and for Vance is 0.82. Carter again ranks second after Kennedy, and Vance is tied for third with Johnson. Given this ranking, we can predict that both Carter and Vance will exhibit high overall flexibility in the area of foreign policy. This finding can be translated into a more concrete form as well. Given the degree of congruence exhibited by Carter and Vance, we can assume that their memory "filters" are quite sensitive and sophisticated in the foreign policy area, so much so that both will be receiving the type of feedback about foreign policy that will enable them to react to situations more flexibly and probably more successfully than many other presidents.

The prediction based on congruence seems rather puzzling in the case of President Carter. Common sense would suggest that Carter, because of his background, should show a low congruence score. In less abstract terms he should exhibit a lack of sensitivity in foreign policy. Carter has never had experience in foreign policy decisions and therefore should be ignorant of many, if not all, foreign policy situations. The data indicate that Carter has a high degree of congruence and therefore is very much in tune with the foreign policy area. The advantage and disadvantage of this model is that we can make the prediction with some comfort, but that we are unable to explain why or how Carter's memory filters reached their current state. Carter's foreign travel and experience in the navy may have made him sensitive to

foreign policy issues. Carter himself may have realized
that he needed to be educated in foreign affairs and may
therefore have surrounded himself with the best teachers he
could find, including Vance and his national security advisor,
Zbigniew Brzezinski. Our framework does not tell us motive
or method, only result.

It has also been predicted that Carter and Vance will exhibit flexible foreign policy behaviors in crisis situations and
that their general behavior will be flexible. We must therefore
ask one final question: over what specifics will they be flexible? In short, what seem to be their major areas of concern?
To answer these questions, we must examine the goals they
have exhibited in the first months of the Carter administration.

Carter has expressed many foreign policy goals—ranging
from promotion of human rights to normalization of relations with Cuba. In all, he articulated ten different goals
during the first six months of his presidency. The three most
frequent were: arms control and a new SALT agreement
(nine), a Middle East peace settlement (seven), and promoting human rights (seven). No other issues appeared more than
three times. If the predictions made about Carter are accurate
and if his foreign policy agenda remains rather consistent, we
can expect flexible behavior from Carter on these issues; and
if a crisis develops surrounding one of these issues, we might
even see a shift in the goals he has discussed. In one sense, the
conventional wisdom has been confirmed. Everyone seems to
have had the impression that Carter is interested primarily in
human rights, the Middle East, and arms control; this has
been confirmed, even if the ordering of those priorities was
not exact.

Vance discussed only three different goals during his first
six months. In this sense, he is very similar to Kissinger, discussing specific policies much more than the goals to which
those policies were directed. Tied for first place with six
occurrences were the goals of a Middle East peace and arms

control. Third, with only a single codable mention, was the promoting of human rights. It is difficult if not impossible, therefore, to speak with any confidence of the types of goals Vance will espouse in the future or what changes will take place in the goals he has already expressed.

It will take several years to see whether the predictions made for Carter and Vance are accurate. One thing can be said however: the predictions are based on a rather novel model; the predictions, if proved accurate, will give further support to the utility of the research framework. Before concluding, it might be useful to reflect for a moment on what conclusions can be drawn from this research.

The Arch and the Tunnel: Implications for Further Study

It was suggested at the outset that a framework of analysis could be constructed to investigate the impact of individual memory on the foreign policy process. Success in this task should allow us to raise this framework from a mere framework to the rarified atmosphere of theory. I demanded that the framework be able to predict rigorously the likely degree of flexibility that a decision-maker will exhibit—without indulging in post hoc analysis of private papers or extensive psychobiography.

Although the exact contribution of the framework and the hypothesis testing are debatable, one thing seems clear. It is possible to discuss in a predictive fashion the degree to which a given decision-maker is likely to change his goals, policies, and referents. Having established a method of comparing individuals across cases, different techniques such as psychobiography take on a new meaning. In fact, psychobiographical materials can now be used as explanation rather than as mere description.

Another result of this theory building and hypothesis testing is to challenge a myth that has plagued foreign policy research for some time. As has been demonstrated, one need *not* be a psychologist to discuss psychological variables. Once a framework has been established, therefore, it is possible to begin to create a cumulative body of knowledge. This research also challenges the myth that individual-level variables in foreign policy are so particular as to be not investigatable in a general and comparative way. Many of the elusive concepts that have been associated with the individual decision-maker are elusive not because they are particular but because we have for far too long accepted the notion that a concept such as memory cannot be operationalized and therefore cannot be investigated. Memory itself may be too broad to operationalize, but elements of memory can in fact be identified, defined, and operationalized.

The theory can be operationalized. However, as with any new concept, the operationalization is at times difficult. Problems arise in empirically investigating concepts such as crisis, failure, and memory and can make the less stouthearted or less foolhardy shy away from the project. However, in every area someone must make a "leap of faith" and hope that he can find a foothold somewhere in the abyss before he encounters utter failure. Fortunately, rank-order correlations of 0.7 and above provide such a foothold.

Since many of the concepts used here were defined and operationalized for the first time in this study, many of the definitions and the data collection techniques remain relatively unrefined. During the course of the research, several improvements suggested themselves for future research. These improvements range from the mundane, such as shortening the time period of editorial sampling for failure determination, to the more significant, such as the redefinition of past, present, and future referents. Such redefinitions would have actually increased the correlations, because it appears that what I defined originally as present was far too limited a period. Our operational definition of present referent was those cognitive objects that occurred during the sample period. Thus, a cognitive object that occurred during the pre-crisis period but was mentioned during the post-crisis period was considered past. In further research, the definition of present will be expanded to include both sample periods. A quick analysis of the current data using this new definition indicates that the rank-order correlations would be increased.

As the research progressed, other shortcomings were discerned, not the least of which were that information about presidential reading material was virtually inaccessible and that other sampling techniques had to be employed in order to make a determination of failure. As this information becomes available, it will be possible to check the sample.

In addition to the difficulties of measuring failure, one cannot overlook the difficulties of measuring crisis. One other scholar has made a serious attempt to operationalize crisis, and even that attempt has been shown to be somewhat judgmental. We attempted to adapt Brewer's scheme but to reduce the amount of judgment involved in determining crisis. Finally, the coding scheme employed for determining goals, policies, and referents was novel, even though it did borrow from other data collection techniques. During the research, it was discovered that the twenty-two-fold *WEIS* categorization of behavior was too reductionist and that the data required a simpler, fivefold classification of behavior. It was also discovered that the modal method of determining dominant types of referents was inferior to an approach that utilized a general mean for each sample period. This method conforms more closely to the assumption that our unit of analysis is the decision-maker rather than the speech.

Having indicated some of the advantages and shortcomings of the theory and its operationalizations, we must now take inventory of what has been found in the process and where such discoveries may lead in the future.

Findings

The data have generally supported the notion that the aspects of memory we identified initially are crucial. More specifically, we have identified two predictive variables—referents and congruence. By examining the types of referents that a decision-maker employs we can and have predicted whether he is likely to change his goals, policies, and referents after experiencing a crisis failure. More abstractly, we now have some idea about differential sensitivity to negative feedback based on certain profile variables that are in turn related to the state of an individual's perceptual filters at any given point. The same is true for congruence, especially in terms of overall change and change in goals. However, a positive relationship does not exist for congruence and policies and congruence and referents, respectively. Further research is required to explain this finding. However, congruence also seems to be a reliable indicator of the state of an individual's perceptual filters and their relationship to the processing of negative feedback.

The research leads to speculation about the nature of the perceptual filters themselves. The more current the filters and the more congruent, the more the decision-maker may be testing reality; and the more he tests reality, the greater the likelihood that he will respond quickly to changes in his operational environment. This speculation does imply both causation and a certain psychological prejudice (which has been studiously avoided throughout the entire research). However, there is enough evidence to suggest that a mechanism of this sort might be operating.

Other results need to be discussed. As the data were collected, some interesting facts emerged about crisis itself and individual's reactions to crisis. Perhaps the most compelling in this regard was the pattern of frequencies of foreign policy–related statements before and after a crisis. As already mentioned, the frequency in almost all cases goes down after a crisis (a finding that replicates previous research).[1] One can, therefore, offer the hypothesis that decision-makers will make fewer foreign policy statements after a crisis.

Not all of the findings were as encouraging as originally

hoped. Several of the hypotheses remain untested, especially those that refer to spatial referents. The data simply did not allow us to test them. Perhaps this is due to certain generational forces, i.e., since the end of World War II, all presidents have had to interest themselves in foreign policy. Therefore, they and their secretaries of state would use a predominance of foreign referents. One way to test this hypothesis would be to sample presidents and secretaries of state from an earlier period in our history (when, presumably, foreign policy was not as salient) and to see whether they, too, exhibited a predominance of foreign referents. A similar situation occurs when one discusses future referents. At this time it is impossible to determine whether the recent leaders of the United States were not forward-looking to any great degree or whether all leaders tend to deal with the past and the present and to leave the future alone.

One rather surprising finding also needs to be mentioned. Initially, we believed that the positive or negative affect attached to a referent might be rather important to a decision-maker. But this was not the case, since the individuals involved rarely if ever stated that a given referent was of positive or negative affect. In short, the dimensions of referent that we termed positive and negative may not exist as we defined them; even if they do, they do not appear to have an impact on our ability to predict the behavior of a decision-maker.

In conclusion, the findings are encouraging. Two of the general hypotheses relating congruence and referent type to degree of flexibility were testable, and the tests that were performed support the hypotheses. In two cases a specific test produced results that were contrary to the hypothesized relationship, but these specific results, which tested the relationship between congruence and policy theme and between congruence and change referents, were overshadowed by the general results involving congruence and overall behavior change and congruence and change in goal themes.

Research, if successful, should indicate avenues of further investigation. No research is ever a stopping point; rather, it should be a way station on the road to further intellectual endeavor. Have we set any new directions, or have we at least indicated that some directions are unprofitable for future work?

As has been shown, the framework with which I began can be usefully employed to compare and contrast U.S. foreign policy decision-makers. It may be profitable to include presidents and secretaries of state who held office before World War II, and if other constraints can be overcome, to include other foreign policy decision-makers, such as secretaries of defense and secretaries of treasury. By increasing the number of individuals in the study, it may be possible to test hypotheses that could not be tested in this first study owing to lack of data.

If sufficient data could be collected, it may be possible to investigate in greater detail the mechanism of prediction that was discovered, to test the interrelationship between referents and congruence, and to assess the relative predictive power of each indicator. It may then be feasible to confirm or disprove the hypotheses on foreign and domestic referents.

The results also lead to the conclusion that it may be desirable to expand the framework to include decision-makers from other cultures. Nothing in the theory itself is culturally bound to the United States or even to the developed world. If appropriate adjustments for determining failure are made, the scheme could be employed to analyze any leader who has an interest in foreign policy. The practical problems of language, logistics, and expense of a cross-national study of this type should not be overlooked, but nothing inherent in the framework itself precludes such an ambitious undertaking; in fact, the results of the first implementation of the scheme tend to encourage rather than discourage this ambition.

Expansion of the scope of the current research, of course,

is not the only implication of the study. The results indicate that the individual is particularistic only if one does not have objective measures by which to compare seemingly "unpatterned" behavior. In fact, they show that top-level foreign policy decision-makers in the United States do tend toward certain patterns of particularistic behavior. If this were not so, then all our hypothesized relationships could not have been supported. As we have also indicated, the notion that in large developed industrial countries individual variables are less important than other variables is a hypothesis that needs further study. In fact, we have illustrated that individuals who have occupied the same roles manifest a marked difference in their behavior and that this difference is at least partly predictable by reference to certain indicators. These indicators are *not* in fact role indicators at all but are constructed from idiosyncratic variables. These indicators—to the degree that they predict behavior—force us to the conclusion that even though a particular memory or filter may be idiosyncratic to a decision-maker, enough similarity exists in the composition and action of these filters to allow general statements about the probable effect of these on the behavior of a class of individuals. It is no longer enough to claim that memory is somehow important to the foreign policy process and then go on to do research that ignores this important variable. As we have demonstrated, it is possible to investigate these variables in a rigorous way and to draw conclusions based on our research. We still must refine our concepts and our definitions, but the first step has been taken. These variables are subject to investigation by political scientists and not just by psychologists. They are important predictors of behavioral change and should not be ignored. They can be analyzed comparatively, and we can make these comparisons before a decision-maker is out of office, has died, or has published the memoirs that give us the "real" story of his career.

Thus we are brought full circle. I realize that the intellectual process that has occurred is one in which novel points of view have been used to construct a framework for analysis. The major question remains: is the further development and articulation of these concepts important or interesting in the quest for knowledge and understanding? What we seek is new knowledge, and that can be achieved only by the articulation of our current thought—since unarticulated thought is after all not knowledge.

> Language is to the mind precisely what the arch is to the tunnel. The power of thinking and the power of excavation are not dependent on the words in the one case or on the mason-work in the other; but without these subsidiaries neither could be carried on beyond its rudimentary commencement. Though, therefore, we allow that every movement forward in language must be determined by an antecedent movement forward in thought, still, unless thought be accompanied at each point of its evolutions by a corresponding evolution of language, its further development is arrested.[2]

I have tried to provide a language for the investigation of memory and flexibility.

Appendix: Coding Manual

This coding manual is designed to measure behavior, crisis, and failure in connection with research into foreign policy flexibility. The manual is divided into several parts, *Make Sure You Read Only That Part of the Manual That Refers to Your Assignment.*

Coding the Crisis

If your assignment is the verification of crisis, refer to this section of the manual. *Do not* refer to any other section of this coding manual. Crisis verification procedures will be described below. You have been assigned a period to code from the *New York Times Index* referring to a specific event, which will be coded to determine the degree to which it conforms to our definition of crisis. There are three elements in this definition: high threat, short time, and surprise. Different coding rules apply to each of these elements.

Coding for High Threat

High threat will be coded along three dimensions: the likelihood that a change in the value inventory will occur, the distance into the future that it will occur, and the magnitude of the change that will take place.

In order to make the proper judgment about the variables contained in high threat, *read all the index entries* before attempting to code for high threat. When coding for change in value inventory, the following questions should be asked: (1) is the threat ambiguous? (2) is the threat definite? (3) is the threatening actor committed irrevocably to the action? If the answer to all three questions is yes, enter the letter *H* on the proper line of the coding sheet. If the answer to two questions is yes, enter *M* on the coding sheet. If the answer to only one question is yes, enter *L* on the coding sheet. If the data do not allow you to answer all three questions, enter the question letter *A* or *B* or *C* on the coding sheet followed by an asterisk.

When coding for the time dimension in terms of high threat, a judgment must be made about when the loss of the valued item will probably occur. If the deprivation will occur within a six-month period beginning with the first sample date, enter *S* on the coding sheet. If the deprivation will not occur until at least six months after the first date of the sample, enter *L* on the coding sheet.

When coding for the magnitude of a threat, a determination must be made as to the probable costs to the United States of the threat if it were successful. If the cost would be in excess of one million dollars, enter *H* on the coding sheet. If the cost involves the loss of United States bases or the employment of the armed forces, enter *H* on the coding sheet. If the costs involve the destruction of major United States economic or trade programs, enter *H* on the coding sheet. If no information is available, enter an asterisk on the coding sheet. If mention is made of the "loss" of an ally or the "subjugation" of a population, this cost will be considered high, and an *H* will be entered on the coding sheet. If the costs involved do not meet any of these criteria, enter an *L* on the coding sheet.

Coding for Short Time

Short time is "real" or "clock" time that is likely to elapse before the situation will change so as to require new approaches and decisions. Short time is determined along two dimensions, complexity and clock time.

When coding for complexity, a determination will be

made as to the number of tasks involved in the situation and the number of United States actors and organizations involved. If the number of tasks to be performed is greater than four or the number of organizations is greater than three, enter *S* on the coding sheet. If the number of tasks is less than four, enter *L* on the coding sheet. In reference to the Cuban missle crisis, for example, you discover that the following agencies were involved: the presidential staff, the Defense Department, the State Department, U.S. mission to the UN, the CIA, and the U.S. Navy. You also discover that the following tasks had to be performed in the context of the situation: informing the USSR of U.S. intentions, organizing the Cuban blockade, calling for a meeting of the Security Council, informing the American public, and mobilizing the national guard. This would be considered short time, since both the organizations involved and the tasks to be performed exceed the necessary level to be considered *S*.

Coding for Surprise

Special coding rules will apply in order to code for surprise. *Code only the designated three-week period for a determination of surprise.* Check all appropriate headings within the index for mention of the situation under study. The situation must be mentioned directly and unambiguously. If no direct mention of the situation is made during the three week period in question, enter an *S* on the coding sheet. If mention of the situation is made, enter an *A* on the coding sheet. *Remember: The reference to the situation must be direct.* For example, a reference to possible trouble in Europe is not to be considered a direct reference to the building of the Berlin Wall.

For the entire period under study, a list must be maintained of all index entries that were utilized in making judgments about crisis. This list will be in chronological order and contain the following information: (1) date, (2) page number, (3) Index heading, (4) entry used for determination of high threat, short time, surprise.

Example: You have been coding for crisis vis-à-vis Korea, on the date of October 15, 1950; you find an entry on page 873 under a heading of Korean War. The information in this entry refers to all three dimensions of crisis. The entry on the list would be written as follows:

10/15/50, 873, Korean War, 1, 2, 3.

Failure

This section concerns only those coders who have been assigned to failure verification procedures. *Do not* refer to any other section of this coding manual. Failure verification procedures will be described below.

You have been assigned a series of dates around a particular crisis. You are to identify and code all editorial columns on those dates that refer to the crisis in question. *Read the entire editorial before you attempt to code it.* The purpose of this coding scheme is to determine the degree of agreement or disagreement of the newspaper with the actions of the leaders under study.

After you have read the editorial, you must identify the key opinion(s) within it. Editorials may contain one or more opinions, and care should be taken to identify and enter on the coding sheet all opinions contained within the editorial being coded. Each opinion must contain a verb and an object (target). The object, or target, must be either the president, the secretary of state, or an official representative of the executive branch of the federal government. Care should be taken to distinguish between opinion and suggestion. Suggestion is the newspaper's best judgment on what ought to be done. Opinion is the newspaper's evaluation of what others have been doing. Enter each opinion in quotations marks on separate lines of the coding sheet.
Example:

> The United States has taken an overdue first step toward restoring normal economic relations with Cuba. . . . Prime

Minister Castro could facilitate restoration [of diplomatic ties] if he would call off Cuba's reckless propaganda drive in the United Nations and elsewhere in behalf of the discredited Marxist Puerto Rican independence movement.

The important thing, however, is that the necessary thaw has begun; the measures announced yesterday are a welcome ingredient in the process. [*New York Times,* Aug. 22, 1975]

In this editorial excerpt, the only opinion relative to the United States would be entered on the coding sheet in the following manner: "the measures announced yesterday [by the U.S.] are a welcome ingredient." The passage about Castro's propaganda actions is a suggestion and not an opinon and will not be coded.

Referents and Themes

This section is only for those who are coding referents and themes. *Do not* refer to any other section of the coding manual. The method we will use for coding referent and theme is described below.

Referent is defined as the cognitive object or event used by the leader in relation to a current situation. Every referent within the speech or news account will be coded. It will be entered on the coding sheet in quotation marks.

Referent can also be coded along a temporal dimension: past, present, or future. A past referent is a referent that occurred before the first day of the sample period. A present referent is one that occurs during the sample period. A future referent is one that occurs or is likely to occur after the sample period.

Determinations can also be made as to whether a referent is foreign or domestic. Foreign referents are those that have border-crossing implications or that occurred completely without the participation of the United States. A domestic referent is an event that occurred primarily within the United States and did not directly involve a foreign (non-U.S.) actor.

Thus the stock market crash of 1929 would be domestic, but the Cuban missile crisis would be foreign.

Referent can also be coded for the positive or negative feelings a decision-maker has about a referent. If the referent is viewed as a good example that should be repeated, the referent is considered positive; if the referent is considered a mistake not to be repeated, the referent is negative.

Coding the Referent

After determinations have been made as to the temporal, spacial, and affective dimensions of a referent, the information will be entered on the coding sheet in the following manner. First, the referent itself will be entered in quotation marks. On the same line of the coding sheet you will enter first whether the referent is past, present (pres), or future (fut). After entering that information, enter either foreign (for) or domestic (dom). This entry will be followed by the positive or negative dimension—enter either a minus sign or a positive sign. If any of the information is unavailable, enter an asterisk in the section of the coding sheet.

Example: during the Cuban misile crisis, the president speaks
  of the necessity to avoid another Munich
Code: "Munich," past, for. -
Example: president mentions the Spanish-American War during Tet offensive
Code: "Spanish-American War," past, for, *

Congruence

In addition to coding for the type of referent itself, we can also code for congruence—the degree of agreement between a referent and the subject matter of a particular section of a speech or news report. The subject matter of the report or situation can be analyzed along a number of dimensions. These dimensions are: regionality, foreign-domestic, temporal, United States involvement, policy type, and issue.

When coding for congruence, the coder will make a separate determination for each variable and enter the information separately on the coding sheet. In terms of regionality, one would ask whether the referent and the subject are based in the same geographical region. In terms of foreign-domestic, we must determine whether the referent and the subject are both domestic or foreign. The temporal dimension refers to agreement as to time. If the referent and subject are both past, present, or future, there is agreement. As for U.S. involvement, the question is whether the United States was a direct participant in both situations or uninvolved in both situations. Policy type refers to the type of policy that is usually associated with a referent and theme and the degree of agreement between them. Is the policy type military, or economic, or diplomatic, and do the type of policies associated with the referent and subject agree? Issue is the subject matter over which actors interact. This issue can be very broad or very specific. Care must be taken to determine from the context of the unit being coded what the issue is and whether that agrees with the issue related to the referent.

Coding for Congruence

The subject matter of a unit being coded may have more than one referent. In coding for congruence, each referent is to be coded separately in relation to the subject. Enter the referent and the subject in quotation marks on the coding sheet. Thus if a president is speaking of Korea and uses Munich as a referent, first enter the referent and then the subject. Thus the line of the coding sheet would read "Munich," "Korea." Below the entry of the referent and subject, information on the agreement or disagreement will be entered on the next six lines. If the referent and subject agree, enter *A* on the proper line. If the referent and subject do not agree, enter *D* on the proper line. The order of appearance will be as follows: Line 1 regionality, Line 2 foreign-domestic, Line 3 temporal, Line 4 United States involvement, Line 5 policy type, Line 6 issue. Thus if we use the example given earlier and the information supplied in the coding source tells us that both situations referred to "global" security, the congruence coding would be as follows:

"Munich," "Korea"
1. *D*
2. *A*
3. *D*
4. *D*
5. *D*
6. *A*

Goal Theme

Goal theme is the desired "future" state that a decision-maker is seeking. In short, it is the "what" of foreign policy. In order to code for goal theme, it is necessary to read completely the source being coded before coding is to begin. The coding of goal theme is done in the following manner. After a coding source has been completely examined, go back and review each paragraph. A determination will then be made as to the goal theme(s) for each paragraph. Where possible, enter the direct quote that contains the goal theme on the coding sheet. Where this is not possible, enter a paraphrased quote. If entering a paraphrased quote, retain as much of the original wording as possible. If entering a paraphrased quote, enter the direct quote that contains the policy goal. Thus if entering a goal theme that seems unclear by itself, paraphrasing of other parts of the paragraph is acceptable as *additional information. Remember, always retain as much information as possible, and <u>do not</u> leave out the verbatim account of the specific goal theme.*

Policy Themes

Since referents are the cognitive objects referred to by a decision-maker and goal themes are the desired future state sought by the leader, policy themes are the conditional statements or the practical efforts used by the leader to gain the goals mentioned. Policy themes are usually found in conditional statements and contain transitive (action) verbs.

Remember: policy themes are the means employed or advocated by a decision-maker. They are therefore the "how" of foreign policy. These means can vary from very cooperative means to very conflictful or even violent means. Once a coding source has been read completely, a determination of the policy themes contained within it will be coded. A policy theme must contain a verb or verb phrase and the direct object of the verb in question. A distinction will also be made as to whether the means is merely suggested or is in in actual use. Therefore, if the policy theme is suggested or proposed, the word indicating suggestion or proposal will be entered on the coding sheet.

Examples:

1. The United States should send economic aid to Poland.
   Code: "should send economic aid to Poland"
2. Today I have sent 200 technical advisors to Korea.
   Code: "I have sent 200 technical advisors to Korea."
3. In order to protect our position in the Middle East, I have sent the secretary of state to enter into peace negotiations.
   Code: "have sent the secretary of state to enter into peace negotiations"

Any source being coded can have more than one policy theme; make sure, therefore, to code *all* policy themes. Policy themes are action-oriented either at the present time or potentially. Therefore, a statement that Castro is a "nasty man" may tell us something about that leader's view of Castro, but that statement alone does not contain a policy theme. However, if the statement was, "Castro is a nasty man, and therefore I have declared a trade embargo against Cuba," it would be codable because the trade embargo is an action. A second point of clarification is useful at this point. If the statement read, "Castro is a nasty man and if he doesn't behave I will subject Cuba to a trade embargo," this statement should also be coded, making sure to include the "will" to indicate the action has not yet occurred.

If a statement is discovered that seems to have a policy theme but the exact nature of the policy theme is unclear, it should also be coded. In a variant of the example given above, the leader may have said, "Castro is a nasty man, and if he does not behave we will make life difficult for him." The phrase, "we will make life difficult for him," should be retained on the coding sheet as a policy theme if no other more detailed information is available within that coding source. *Remember to code the report or section of the report that contains the greatest detail.* Thus if in paragraph one the president says we will be nasty and in paragraph three he indicates how he intends to be nasty, code the statement contained in paragraph three.

Notes

Chapter 1

1. Samuel Eliot Morison, *The Oxford History of the American People* (New York: Oxford University Press, 1965), p. 366.

2. Letter from Thomas Jefferson to James Madison, December 29, 1787.

3. J. D. Richardson, ed., *Messages and Papers of the Presidents 1789-1902,* vol. 1 (Washington D.C., 1917), pp. 309-312.

4. Letter from Thomas Jefferson to J. B. Colvin, September 20, 1810.

5. Ole R. Holsti, "The Belief System and National Images: A Case Study," *The Journal of Conflict Resolution* 6 (1962): 244-252.

6. Ibid.

7. See Chapter 2, pp. 71-24.

Chapter 2

1. C. N. Cofer and M. H. Appley, *Motivation Theory and Research* (New York: John Wiley and Sons, 1964), p. 5

2. Harold and Margaret Sprout, *Foundations of International Politics* (Princeton, N.J.: D. Van Nostrand Co., 1962), pp. 48-49.

3. John P. Lovell, *Foreign Policy in Perspective* (New

York: Holt, Rinehart and Winston, 1970), pp. 9-10.

4. Karl W. Deutsch, *Nerves of Government* (New York: Free Press, 1966), p. 101.

5. Ole Holsti, R. C. North, and Richard Brody, "Perception and Action in the 1914 Case," in *Quantitative International Politics,* ed. J. David Singer (New York: Free Press, 1968), p. 128.

6. Raymond F. Hopkins and Richard W. Mansbach, *Structure and Process in International Politics* (New York: Harper and Row, 1973), p. 3.

7. Ibid., p. 156.

8. Patrick M. Morgan, *Theories and Approaches to International Politics* (San Remo, Calif.: Consensus Publishers, 1972), pp. 113-114.

9. Deutsch, *Nerves of Government,* pp. 128-129.

10. Sprout, *Foundations of International Politics,* p. 105.

11. Charles F. Hermann, "Policy Classification: A Key to the Comparative Study of Foreign Policy," in *The Analysis of International Politics,* ed. James N. Rosenau, Vincent Davis, and Maurice A. East (New York: Free Press, 1972), p. 72.

12. Roger Hilsman, *The Politics of Policy Making in Defense and Foreign Affairs* (New York: Harper and Row, 1971), p. 3.

13. See Susan B. Jones and J. David Singer, *Beyond Conjecture in International Politics* (Itasca, Ill.: F. E. Peacock, 1972). Jones and Singer contain only 15 of 158 abstracts pertaining to decision making and perception. Also see Patrick J. McGowan and Howard B. Shapiro, *The Comparative Study of Foreign Policy* (Beverly Hills, Calif.: Sage Publishing Co., 1973). McGowan and Shapiro include 19 decision-making studies of a total of 200 studies cited.

14. Sidney Verba, "Assumptions of Rationality and non-Rationality in Models of International Systems," in *The International System: Theoretical Essays,* ed. Klaus Knorr

and Sidney Verba (Princeton, N.J.: Princeton University Press, 1955).

15. R. C. North and N. Choucri, "Background Conditions to the Outbreak of the First World War," *Peace Research Society (International) Papers*, no. 9 (1968), pp. 125-137; see also R. C. North, "Perception and Action in the 1914 Crisis," *Journal of International Affairs* 21 (1967): 103-122.

16. Ole Hosti, "The 1914 Case," *American Political Science Review* 58 (June 1965): 365-378.

17. Holsti, North, and Brody, "Perception and Action in the 1914 Case," pp. 123-158.

18. M. D. Wallace, "Power Status and International War," *Journal of Peace Research* 8 (1971): 23-36.

19. M. A. East, "Status Discrepancy and Balance in the International System: An Empirical Analysis," in Rosenau, Davis, and East, *Analysis of International Politics*, pp. 299-316.

20. Joseph H. de Rivera, *The Psychological Dimension of Foreign Policy* (Columbus, Ohio: Merrill, 1968).

21. Irving Janis, *Victims of Groupthink* (Boston: Houghton Mifflin Co., 1972).

22. Graham T. Allison, *Essence of Decision* (Boston: Little Brown and Co., 1971).

23. See Glenn D. Paige, "Comparative Case Analysis of Crisis Decisions: Korea and Cuba," in *International Crises: Insights from Behavioral Research*, ed. Charles Hermann (New York: Free Press, 1968), p. 276.

24. Richard C. Snyder, H. W. Bruck, and Burton Sapin, "The Decision-Making Approach to the Study of International Politics," in *International Politics and Foreign Policy*, ed. James N. Rosenau (New York: Free Press, 1969), p. 201.

25. Ibid., p. 202.

26. Ibid., p. 203.

27. Ibid.

28. James N. Rosenau, *The Scientific Study of Foreign*

Policy (New York: Free Press, 1971), pp. 270-271.

29. Ibid., p. 263.

30. Morgan, *Theories and Approaches*, pp. 113-114.

31. Ernest May, "The Nature of Foreign Policy: The Calculated versus the Axiomatic," *Daedalus* 91 (Fall 1962): pp. 653-667.

32. Sprout, *Foundations of International Politics*, pp. 48-49.

33. John P. Lovell, *Foreign Policy in Perspective* (New York: Holt, Rinehart and Winston, 1970), pp. 9-10.

34. Holsti, North, and Brody, "Perception and Action."

35. Hermann, "Policy Classification."

36. Paige, "Comparative Case Analysis."

37. James A. Robinson and Richard C. Snyder, "Decision-making in International Politics," in *International Behavior: A Social Psychological Analysis*, ed. Herbert C. Kelman (New York: Holt, Rinehart and Winston, 1965), p. 442.

38. Alexander M. George, David K. Hall, and William E. Simons, *The Limits of Coercive Diplomacy, Laos, Cuba, Vietnam* (Boston: Little Brown and Co., 1971), p. ix.

39. Allison, *Essence of Decision.*

40. James M. McCormick, "Evaluating Models of Crisis Behavior: Some Evidence from the Middle East," *International Studies Quarterly* 19 (March 1975): 17-45.

41. Rosenau, *Scientific Study of Foreign Policy*, p. 113.

42. See Rosenau's discussion of development, size, and regime type. Ibid., pp. 111-116.

43. Ibid., p. 113.

44. Ibid., p. 108.

45. Ibid.

46. Alexander George, "The Operational Code: A Neglected Approach to the Study of Political Leaders and Decision-Makers," *International Studies Quarterly* 12 (June 1969).

47. Hermann, *International Crises*, pp. 6-9.

48. Ibid., p. 9.

49. Robinson and Snyder, "Decision-making in International Politics."

50. Paige, "Comparative Case Analysis."

51. Ibid.

52. Thomas L. Brewer, "Issue and Context Variations in Foreign Policy," *Journal of Conflict Resolution* 17 (March 1973): 89-114.

53. May, "The Nature of Foreign Policy."

54. Ibid.

55. Ibid.

56. Fred. I. Greenstein, *Personality and Politics* (Chicago: Markham Publishing Co., 1969).

57. de Rivera, *Psychological Dimension,* p. 131.

58. Rosenau, *Scientific Study of Foreign Policy,* p. 263.

59. Ibid., pp. 263-264.

60. Ibid., p. 264.

61. Greenstein, *Personality and Politics,* pp. 46-56.

62. Emphasis and footnotes deleted. Ibid., p. 56.

63. William Wilcox, *Portrait of a General* (New York: Alfred A. Knopf, 1964).

64. Daniel Levinson, "Role Personality and Social Structure in Organizational Setting," *Journal of Abnormal and Social Psychology* 58 (1959): 170-180.

65. Robinson and Snyder, "Decision-making in International Politics," p. 442.

66. Emphasis deleted. Greenstein, *Personality and Politics,* p. 54.

67. Ibid., pp. 50-51.

68. See Muzafer Sherif, "The Concept of Reference Groups in Human Relations," in *Group Relations at the Crossroads,* ed. Muzafer Sherif and M. O. Wilson (New York: Harper and Row, 1963), p. 211; see also Stanley Budner, "Intolerance of Ambiguity as a Personality Variable," *Journal of Personality* 30: 29-50.

69. Paige, "Comparative Case Analysis," p. 47.

70. Ibid.

71. Robert Kennedy, *Thirteen Days* (New York: W. W. Norton & Co., 1971), pp. 15-17.

72. Deutsch, *Nerves of Government,* pp. 92-93.

73. Ibid., pp. 128-129.

74. Ibid.

75. Hans Morgenthau, *Politics among Nations,* 4th ed. (New York: Alfred A. Knopf, 1966).

76. Allison, *Essence of Decision.*

77. Paige, "Comparative Case Analysis."

78. de Rivera, *Psychological Dimension.*

79. Greenstein, *Personality and Politics.*

80. Snyder, Bruck, and Sapin, "The Decision-Making Approach to the Study of International Politics."

81. Holsti, "The Belief System and National Images," p. 251.

82. Deutsch, *Nerves of Government,* p. 258.

83. See Chapter 2, p. 27.

84. See Chapter 2, p. 24.

85. Hopkins and Mansbach, *Structure and Process.*

86. Deutsch, *Nerves of Government.*

87. Holsti, "The Belief System and National Images."

Chapter 3

1. Abraham Kaplan, *Logic of Inquiry* (Scranton, Pa.: Chandler, 1964), p. 198.

2. Holsti, "The Belief System and National Images," p. 246.

3. See Ole R. Holsti, "Cognitive Dynamics and Images of the Enemy: Dulles and Russia," in *Enemies in Politics,* ed. D. J. Finley, Ole R. Holsti, and R. R. Fagen (Chicago: Rand McNally, 1967), p. 28; G. G. Gutierrez, "Dean Rusk and Southeast Asia: An Operational Code Analysis" (Paper prepared for the American Political Science Association 1973 annual meetings), p. 15; see also David S. McLellan, "Comparative Operational Codes of U.S. Secretaries of State: Dean

Acheson" (Paper presented at the Sixty-Fifth Annual Meeting of the American Political Science Association, September 1969), p. 2.

4. See E. E. Azar and J. D. Ben Dak, eds., *International Interactions: Theory and Practice of Events Data* (New York: Gordon and Breach, 1973); see also Thomas L. Brewer, *Foreign Policy Situations,* Sage Professional Papers in International Studies (Beverly Hills, Calif.: Sage Publishing Co., 1972).

5. Hermann, "Policy Classification," pp. 58-79.

6. A second question involves the reliability of the data source. As the research depends upon a version of content analysis, the question of intercoder reliability becomes crucial. For this reason, we will employ only one coder.

7. Hermann, *International Crises,* p. 15.

8. See the following publications by Thomas L. Brewer: "Foreign Policy Process Events: Problems of Concept and Data," in Azar and Ben Dak, *International Interactions;* "Issue and Context Variations in Foreign Policy," pp. 89-114; "Issue Type and Context in American Foreign Policy-Making: An Analysis of Elite Behavior in Sixty-Five European Integration and Atlantic Alliance Cases, 1949-1968" (Ph.D. diss., State University of New York at Buffalo, 1971).

9. Brewer, "Foreign Policy Process Events," p. 68.

10. Emphasis in original. Charles A. McClelland, "International Interaction Analysis: Basic Research and Some Practical Applications," technical report no. 2, Department of International Relations, University of Southern California, 1968, pp. 46-48. It seems reasonable that if the statement just cited can be made about the *New York Times,* the same statement could be made concerning the *New York Times Index.*

11. Stephen Salmore, "National Attributes and Foreign Policy: A Multivariate Analysis" (Ph.D. dissertation, Princeton University, 1972), p. 13.

12. Ithiel de Sola Pool, *The Prestige Papers* (Stanford: Stanford University Press, 1952), p. 1, 8.

13. See Bernard C. Cohen, *The Press and Foreign Policy* (Princeton, N.J.: Princeton University Press, 1963).

14. *Milieu* in this context is equivalent to the definition used by Harold and Margaret Sprout, "Environmental Factors in the Study of International Politics," *Journal of Conflict Resolution* 1 (1957): 309-328.

15. James N. Rosenau, *Public Opinion and Foreign Policy* (New York: Random House, 1964).

16. Ibid., p. 84.

17. Brewer, "Issue and Context Variations," pp. 98-99.

18. See Chapter 3, on operationalizing the intervening variables, pp. 55-58.

19. See Chapter 2, pp. 27-31.

20. Deutsch, *Nerves of Government,* p. 258.

21. Holsti, "The Belief System and National Images," p. 251.

22. Snyder, Bruck, and Sapin, "The Decision-Making Approach to the Study of International Politics," p. 201.

23. Greenstein, *Personality and Politics.*

24. Allison, *Essence of Decision.*

25. See Paige, "Comparative Case Analysis"; and idem, *The Korean Decision* (New York: Free Press, 1968), p. 276.

26. de Rivera, *Psychological Dimension.*

27. Morgenthau, *Politics among Nations.*

28. Dean Rusk, speech before 7th meeting of Southeast Asia Treaty Organization, Bangkôk, Thailand, March 7, 1961.

29. Ibid.

30. Ibid.

31. A unit is defined as any speech, answer, or press release. In cases of major speeches or wide-ranging news conferences, a unit is considered to be those parts of the speech that refer to foreign policy.

32. See Chapter 2, pp. 30-31.

33. Adapted from Hopkins and Mansbach, *Structure and Process,* p. 60.

34. See Chapter 2, p. 31.

35. Dean Rusk, January 31, 1962, closing remarks at OAS meeting in Punta del Este.

36. Charles A. McClelland and Gary D. Hoggard, "Conflict Patterns in the Interactions Among Nations," in Rosenau, *International Politics and Foreign Policy,* pp. 711-724.

37. Ibid., pp. 714-715.

38. The merging of offensive and defensive verbal conflict, although based upon the *WEIS* system, has already been employed by the *Nonstate Actor Project (NOSTAC).* See Richard W. Mansbach, Yale H. Ferguson, and Donald E. Lampert, *The Web of World Politics* (Englewood Cliffs, N.J.: Prentice Hall, 1976).

39. The time periods listed in Table 1 are possibilities only. No definite sample dates can be determined until crisis situations have been verified both as crisis and as failure. This list contains crisis events that have a high probability of being verified. One crisis failure will be used for each postwar presidential administration, save for the Ford administration. This list may be modified slightly to allow for proper crisis verification techniques.

40. Definition of crisis is adapted from Hermann, *International Crises,* pp. 6-17.

41. Charles A. McClelland, "The Beginning, Duration, and Abatement of International Crises: Comparisons in Two Conflict Arenas," in ibid., pp. 83-105.

42. See Paige, "Comparative Case Analysis"; Holsti, "Cognitive Dynamics"; and Hermann, *International Crises.*

43. Adapted from Brewer, "Issue and Context Variations," pp. 92-93.

44. Ibid.

45. Charles F. Hermann, *Crises in Foreign Policy* (Indianapolis: Bobbs-Merrill, 1969), p. 29.

46. J. A. Robinson, "Crisis," in *International Encyclopedia of the Social Sciences,* edited by David L. Sills, 17 vols. (New York: The Macmillan Company and The Free Press, 1968), 3:510-514.

47. J. A. Robinson and R. C. Snyder, "Decision-making in International Politics," p. 440.

48. Brewer, *Foreign Policy Situations,* p. 93.

49. Dan D. Nimmo, *News Gathering in Washington* (New York: Atherton Press, 1964), pp. 185-186.

Chapter 4

1. Hermann, *International Crises: Insights from Behavioral Research,* pp. 6-7.

2. See the following publications by Thomas L. Brewer: "Issue and Context Variations in Foreign Policy," pp. 89-117; "Foreign Policy Process Events: Problems of Concept and Data," in Azar and Ben Dak, *International Interactions: Foreign Policy Situations.*

3. See the discussion of high threat and high salience, Chapter 2, pp. 17-20.

4. One coder was employed for the determination of high threat.

5. See John Gittings, *The Role of the Chinese Army* (London: Oxford University Press, 1967), pp. 4-5. See also Roderick MacFarquhar, *Sino-American Relations 1949-1971* (New York: Praeger, 1972).

6. Harold Vinacki, ed., *A History of the Far East in Modern Times* (New York: Appleton Century Crofts, 1956), p. 714; see also United Nations, General Assembly, document A/1435.

7. Warren I. Cohen, *America's Response to China* (New York: John Wiley and Sons, 1971), p. 205.

8. This measure is judgmental, and to avoid the problem of intercoder reliability only one coder was employed.

9. This measure is generally adapted from the work of Thomas L. Brewer. See the works listed in Chapter 4, note 2.

10. The rule regarding precedent proved unnecessary in the cases we are examining. The only situation in which this problem would have arisen was the intervention of the People's Republic of China in Korea, but there were suffi-

cient U.S.-based precedents to make the argument moot.

11. Cohen, *America's Response to China,* p. 205.

12. Ibid. Emphasis added.

13. The information necessary, i.e., White House subscription lists, were requested from the appropriate federal authorities. After three months of delay and a series of contradictory answers to the researcher and to Rep. Dominick V. Daniels and Sen. Clifford Case, the attempt to obtain this information was abandoned after consultation with several scholars specializing in the media and politics, including Professor John Pollock, Livingston College, and Ben Bagdigian, former editor of the *Washington Post.*

14. Nimmo, *News Gathering in Washington,* p. 187.

15. Karl W. Deutsch, *The Analysis of International Relations* (Englewood Cliffs, N.J.: Prentice-Hall, 1968); see also Gabriel A. Almond, *The American People and Foreign Policy* (New York: Harcourt, Brace, Jovanovich, 1950).

16. Douglass Cater, Jr., *The Fourth Branch of Government* (Boston: Houghton Mifflin, 1959); Cohen, *The Press and Foreign Policy;* James Reston, *The Artillery of the Press* (New York: Harper and Row, 1967).

17. Nimmo, *News Gathering in Washington,* pp. 185-86.

18. From personal communication with Dan D. Nimmo. His opinion was that the *Washington Daily News* tended to be sensational and was therefore irrelevant to the failure sampling used here and that the other newspapers in the sample cover similar opinions.

19. Although the additional fourteen-day period was examined, it was discovered that a ten-day addition was sufficient in order to capture the types of editorials necessary.

20. *New York Herald Tribune,* November 5, 1956.

21. *Washington Post,* August 29, 1961.

22. The *Washington Evening Star* contained all neutral editorials vis-à-vis the administration, and the *New York Times* contained one positive, one negative, and four neutral

editorials.

23. This is analogous to an abstention in the UN. When a member abstains, his vote is not counted as either positive or negative in determining a majority.

24. *New York Herald Tribune,* August 15, 1961.

25. A. F. Lowenthal, *The Dominican Intervention* (Cambridge, Mass.: Harvard University Press, 1972), p. 150.

26. W. Howard Wriggins, "Political Development: Varieties of Political Change and US Policy" in *Foreign Policy in the Sixties,* ed. Roger Hilsman and Robert C. Good (Baltimore: Johns Hopkins Press, 1965), p. 119.

27. Robert Shaplen, *The Road From War* (New York: Harper Colophon Books, 1971), p. 188.

28. Dwight D. Eisenhower, *Waging Peace 1956-1961* (New York: Doubleday, 1965), pp. 88-89.

Chapter 5

1. See Chapter 4, p. 72.

2. Adam B. Ulam, *The Rivals* (New York: Viking Press, 1971), p. 136.

3. Herbert Feis, *From Trust to Terror: The Onset of the Cold War, 1945-1950* (New York: W. W. Norton, 1970), p. 294.

4. *Washington Post,* March 1, 1948.

5. Ibid.

6. Feis, *From Trust to Terror,* p. 294.

7. David Horowitz, *The Free World Colossus* (New York: Hill and Wang, 1965), p. 90.

8. Ibid., pp. 95-96.

9. Richard W. Mansbach and John A. Vasquez, "Issue Politics v. Power Politics" (Paper presented at the New Jersey Political Science Association, April 1976).

10. Cabell Phillips, *The Truman Presidency* (New York: Macmillan, 1966), p. 237.

11. Ole R. Holsti, "The Belief System and National Images: A Case Study," in *International Politics and Foreign*

Policy, ed. James N. Rosenau (New York: Free Press, 1969), p. 549.

12. Harry S. Truman, *Memoirs,* 2 vols. (Garden City, N.Y.: Doubleday, 1956) 2:105.

13. *New York Times,* April 1, 1948.

14. See Chapter 6, p. 107.

15. Merle Miller, *Plain Speaking: An Oral Biography of Harry S. Truman* (New York: Berkley Pub., 1974), p. 254.

16. Joe McCarthy, *The Story of General George Marshall* (Washington: Joe McCarthy, 1952), p. 4.

17. The fact that Kennan discussed the possibility of the situation in Czechoslovakia does not in any way contradict our determination of crisis. See chap. 4. See also George F. Kennan, *Memoirs 1925-1950* (Boston: Little Brown, 1967), pp. 378-379.

18. Erich Hula, "The Evolution of Collective Security under the United Nations Charter," in *Alliance Policy in the Cold War,* ed. Arnold Wolfers (Baltimore: The Johns Hopkins Press), p. 78.

19. Dwight D. Eisenhower, *Waging Peace* (Garden City, N.Y.: Doubleday, 1965), pp. 263-273.

20. Quoted in John Robinson Beal, *John Foster Dulles: 1888-1959* (New York: Harper Brothers, 1959), pp. 333-334.

21. Holsti, "The Belief System and National Images," p. 548.

22. *Wall Street Journal,* July 17, 1958.

23. Raymond L. Garthoff, "The Cold War and the Changing Communist World," in *Foreign Policy in the Sixties,* ed. Roger Hilsman and Robert C. Good (Baltimore: The Johns Hopkins Press, 1965), p. 5.

24. Arthur M. Schlesinger, *A Thousand Days* (Boston: Houghton Mifflin, 1965), pp. 390-391.

25. Benjamin Bradlee, *Conversations with Kennedy* (New York: W. W. Norton, 1975) p. 126.

26. Geoffrey Stern, "Soviet Foreign Policy in Theory and Practice," in *The Foreign Policies of the Powers,* ed. F. S.

Northedge (New York: Free Press, 1974), p. 116.

27. Charles A. McClelland, "The Beginning, Duration, and Abatement of International Crises: Comparisons in Two Conflict Arenas," in Hermann, *International Crises,* pp. 83-105.

28. See, for example, Henry T. Nash, *American Foreign Policy* (Homewood, Ill.: The Dorsey Press, 1973.), p. 68.

29. Schlesinger, *Thousand Days,* p. 383.

30. Ibid., p. 389.

31. McClelland, "The Beginning, Duration, and Abatement of International Crises," p. 105.

32. Robert Shaplen, *The Road from War* (New York: Harper Colophon Books, 1971), pp. 188-189.

33. The personality type exhibited by Johnson is common only with Nixon. The other presidents in the study are different in terms of the Barber scheme of presidential personality. See James David Barber, "The Interplay of Presidential Character and Style: A Paradigm and Five Illustrations," in *Perspectives on the Presidency,* ed. Aaron Wildavsky (Boston: Little, Brown, 1975), p. 69.

34. Ibid., p. 81.

35. Chapter 5, p. 88.

36. Nash, *American Foreign Policy,* p. 68.

37. Gary S. Schiff, "Beyond Disengagement: Conflict Resolution in the Middle East since the 1973 War," *World Affairs* 137 (Winter 1974-1975): 195-205. Quote on p. 201.

38. Fouad Ajami, "Middle East Ghosts," *Foreign Policy,* no. 14 (1974), pp. 91-111. Quote on p. 106.

39. Ibid., p. 110.

40. Jerry Voorhis, *The Strange Case of Richard Milhous Nixon* (New York: Paul S. Eriksson, 1972), p. 278.

41. Richard M. Nixon, *Setting the Course: The First Year* (New York: Funk & Wagnalls, 1970), p. 315.

42. See Chapter 6, pp. 105-106.

43. Gaddis Smith, "Henry A. Kissinger and His Predecessors: A Comparative Rating of American Secretaries of State in the Modern Era, 1914-1976 (Paper presented at the

International Studies Association, February 1976), p. 31.

44. Albert F. Eldridge, Jr., "The Crisis of Authority: The President, Kissinger & Congress (1969-1974)" (Paper presented February 1976), pp. 39-40.

45. Dana Ward, "A Second Look at Kissinger's Impact on American Foreign Policy" (Paper presented at the International Studies Association, February 1976), p. 22.

46. Ibid.

47. Ibid.

Chapter 6

1. See Chapter 3, pp. 37-60.

2. A unit is defined as a particular speech or part of a speech. It can also be all responses to questions on a similar foreign policy subject matter during the course of a news conference or in congressional testimony. Quite often in these cases, an initial question is followed by more specific questions requiring the respondent to give a more specific answer. The entire exchange is considered one unit for coding purposes.

3. Since only one coder was employed, the intercoder reliability score is 1.00.

4. The *New York Times* proved to be an excellent coding source. It tended to carry verbatim transcripts whenever they were obtainable and practical to carry. Other sources—such as the congressional record or State Department bulletins—so seldom were referred to as to be negligible in terms of the overall coding.

5. This type of situation occurred especially under President Nixon. During certain news conferences, almost every question was about the Watergate scandal, and the president, even if he desired to discuss foreign affairs, was not given the opportunity to do so.

6. In reality, there are only nine individuals in the study. However, Dean Rusk is considered as two individuals, since he was secretary of state under two presidents, Kennedy and

Johnson.

7. See McClelland, "The Beginning, Duration, and Abatement of International Crises, pp. 97-100.

8. Adam B. Ulam, *The Rivals: America and Russia since World War II* (New York: Viking Press, 1971), pp. 141-143.

9. Holsti, "The Belief System and National Images," pp. 548-549.

10. See Chapter 3, p. 52. Also see Mansbach, Ferguson, and Lampert, *The Web of World Politics*, pp. 300-317.

11. The formula used for all the rank-order correlations is:

$$\text{rho} = \frac{6\Sigma D^2}{N\,(N^2-1)}$$

Chapter 7

1. See Chapter 6, p. 105.

2. Quoted in Samuel Butler, "Thought and Language," in *The Importance of Language,* ed. Max Black (Englewood Cliffs, N.J.: Prentice-Hall, 1962), pp. 34-35.

Index

*References with n or nn refer to the Notes section of this book.